STEM ADVENTURES

THE AMAZING STORY OF THE COMBUSTION ENGINE

MAX AXIOM
STEM ADVENTURES

by Mari Bolte

illustrated by Pop Art Properties

Consultant:
Margaret Wooldridge, PhD
Arthur F. Thurnau Professor
Departments of Mechanical and Aerospace Engineering
College of Engineering
University of Michigan, Ann Arbor

CAPSTONE PRESS
a capstone imprint

Graphic Library is published by Capstone Press,
1710 Roe Crest Drive, North Mankato, Minnesota 56003
www.capstonepub.com

Library of Congress Cataloging-in-Publication Data
Bolte, Mari.
The amazing story of the combustion engine : Max Axiom STEM adventures / by Mari Bolte ; illustrated by Pop Art Properties.
pages cm.—(Graphic library. STEM adventures.)
Summary: "In graphic novel format, follows Max Axiom as he explains how combustion engines work"—Provided by publisher.
Audience: Grade 4 to 6.
Includes bibliographical references and index.
ISBN 978-1-4765-3103-8 (library binding)
ISBN 978-1-4765-3459-6 (paperback)
ISBN 978-1-4765-3455-8 (eBook PDF)
1. Internal combustion engines—Juvenile literature. 2. Internal combustion engines—Comic books, strips, etc. 3. Graphic novels. I. Pop Art Properties, illustrator. II. Title.
TJ785.B63 2014
621.43—dc23

2013003123

Designer
Ted Williams

Cover Artist
Marcelo Baez

Media Researcher
Wanda Winch

Production Specialist
Eric Manske

Editor
Christopher L. Harbo

Photo Credits: Shutterstock: PHB.cz(Richard Semik), 7, sima, 19

Printed in the United States 5999

TABLE of CONTENTS

SECTION 1 ENGINE BASICS

A visit to an auto show sends super scientist Max Axiom into a full-throttle exploration of the internal combustion engine.

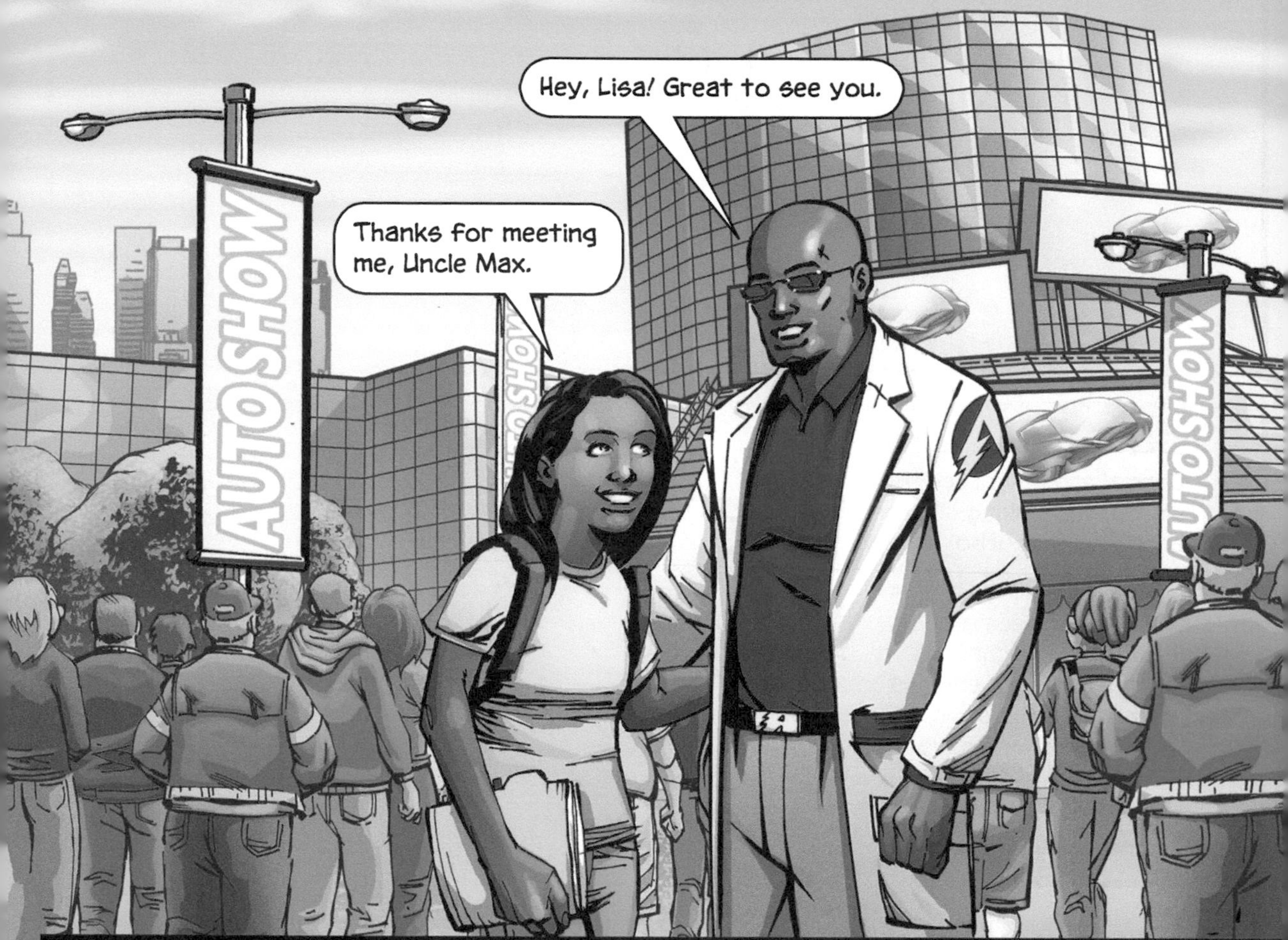
AUTO SHOW
Hey, Lisa! Great to see you.
Thanks for meeting me, Uncle Max.

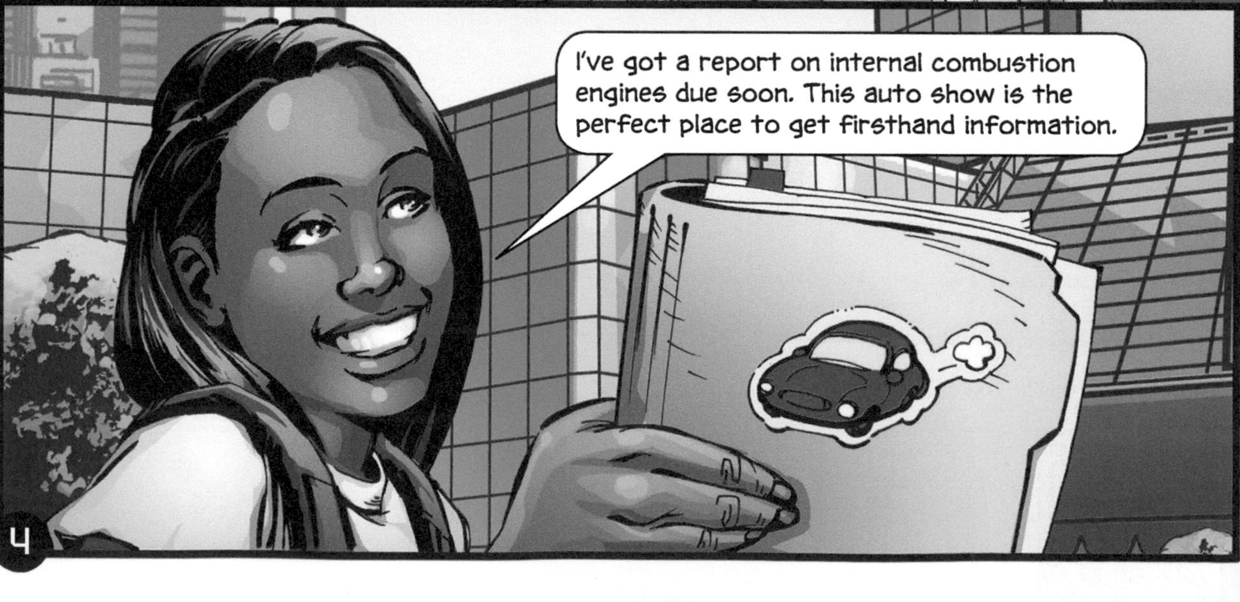
I've got a report on internal combustion engines due soon. This auto show is the perfect place to get firsthand information.

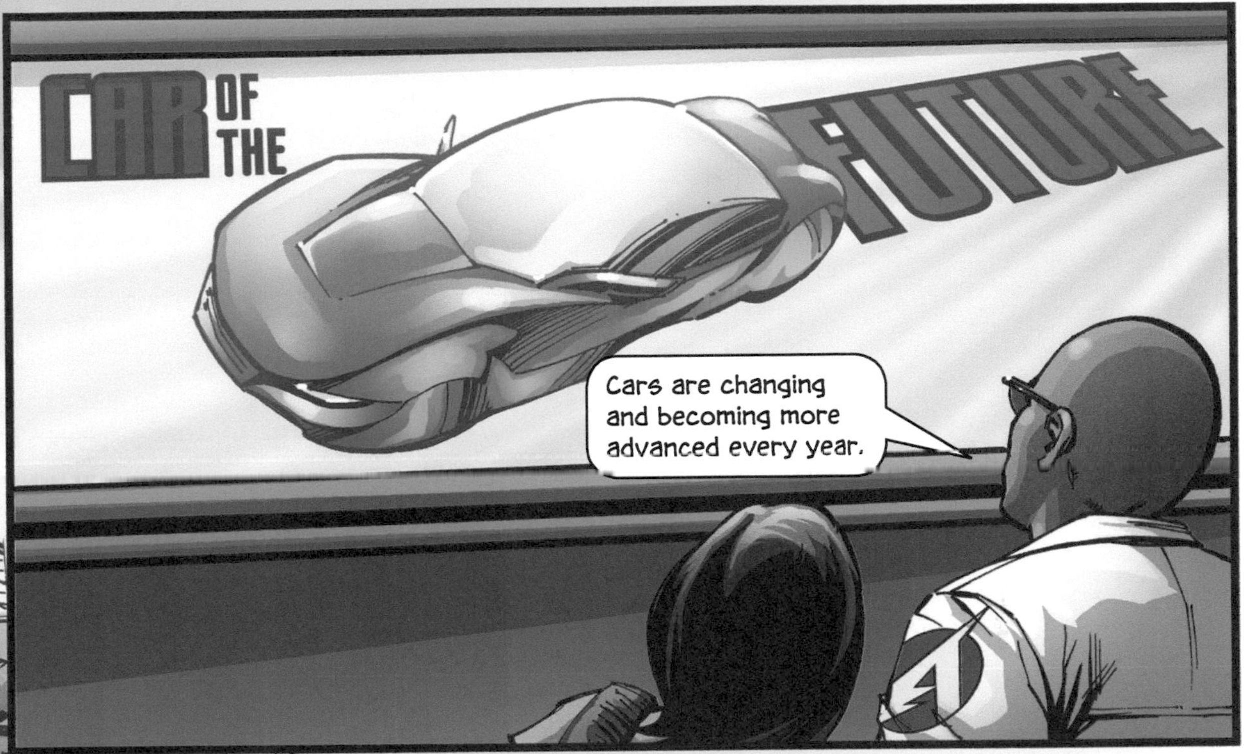
CAR OF THE FUTURE
Cars are changing and becoming more advanced every year.

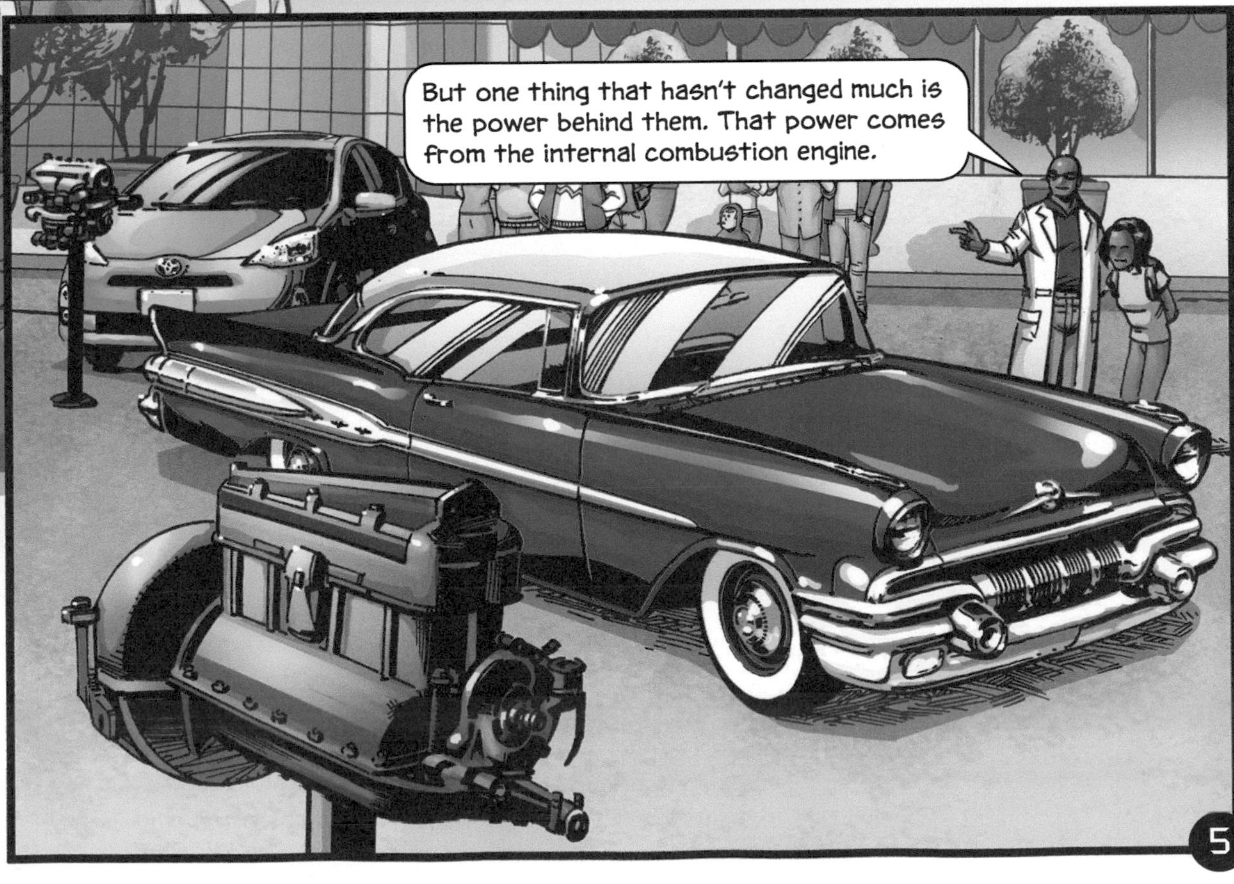
But one thing that hasn't changed much is the power behind them. That power comes from the internal combustion engine.

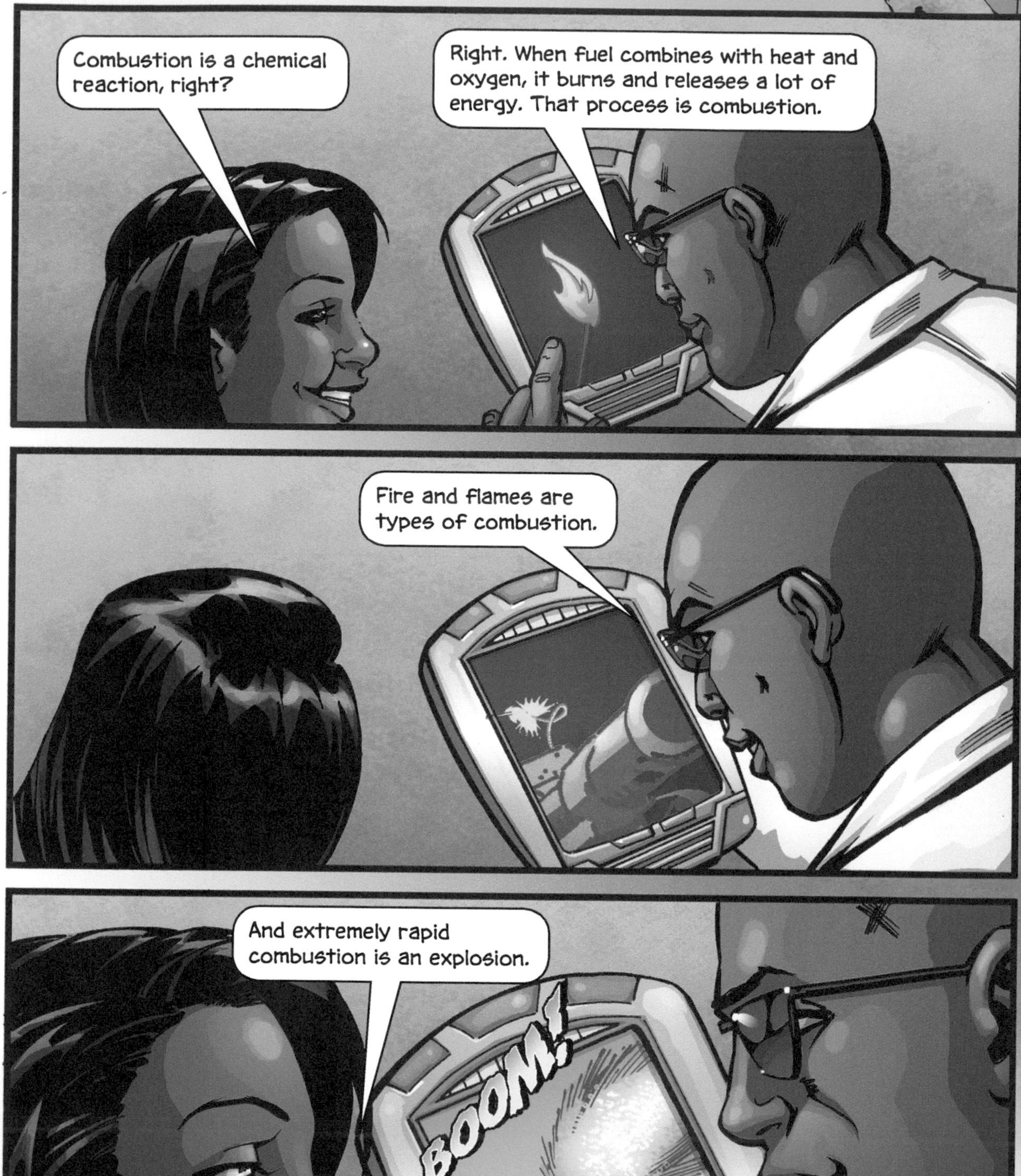
Combustion is a chemical reaction, right?
Right. When fuel combines with heat and oxygen, it burns and releases a lot of energy. That process is combustion.
Fire and flames are types of combustion.
And extremely rapid combustion is an explosion.
BOOM!

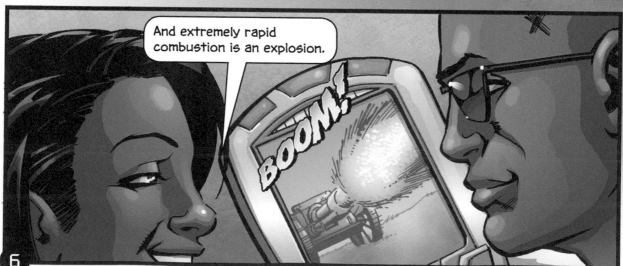

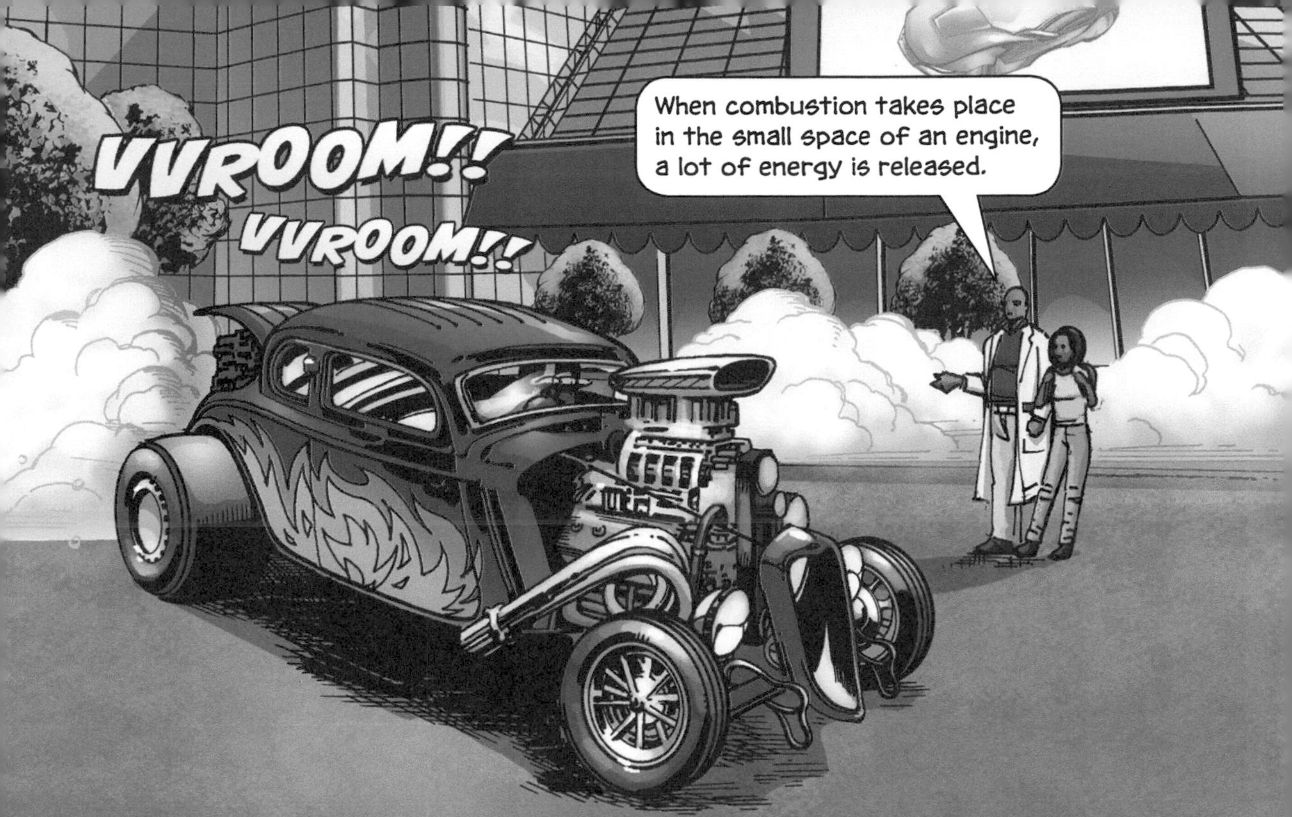
VVROOM!!
VVROOM!!
When combustion takes place in the small space of an engine, a lot of energy is released.

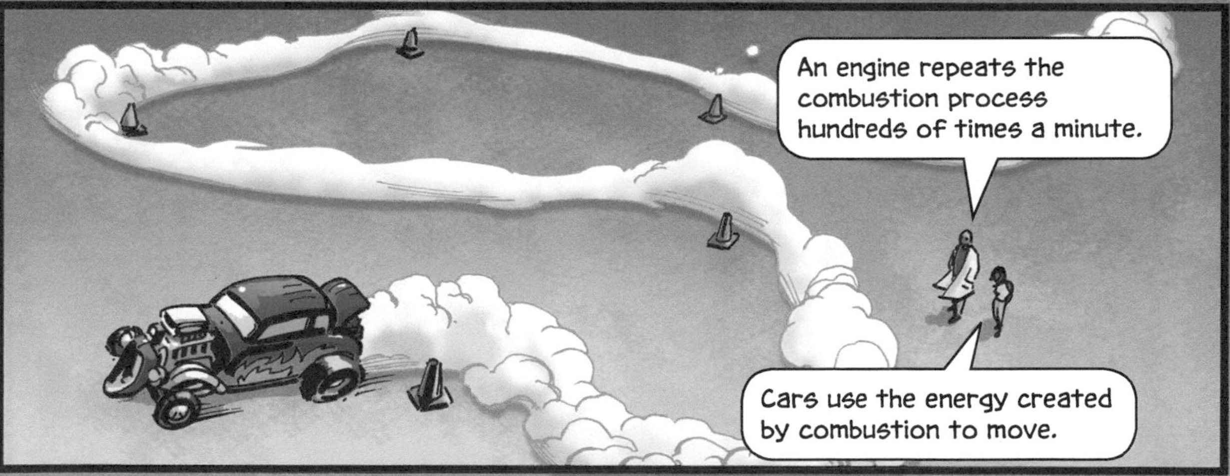
An engine repeats the combustion process hundreds of times a minute.
Cars use the energy created by combustion to move.

EXTERNAL COMBUSTION ENGINES

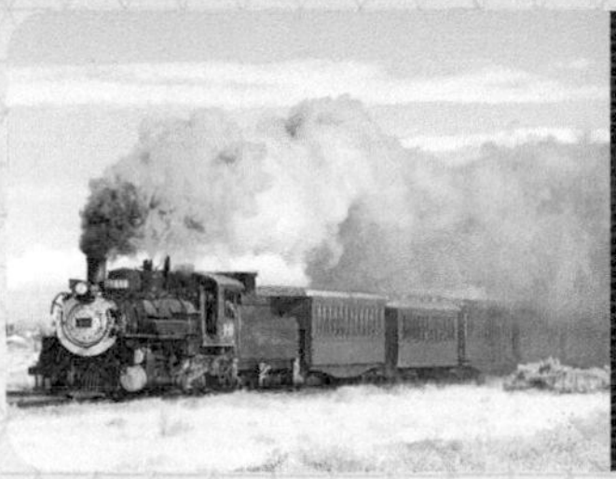

Fuel burns inside the engine during internal combustion. External combustion takes place outside the engine. For example, steam engines are a form of external combustion. Fuel burns outside the engine and is used to create steam. The steam powers the engine. External combustion engines can use fuels such as wood, coal, and oil.

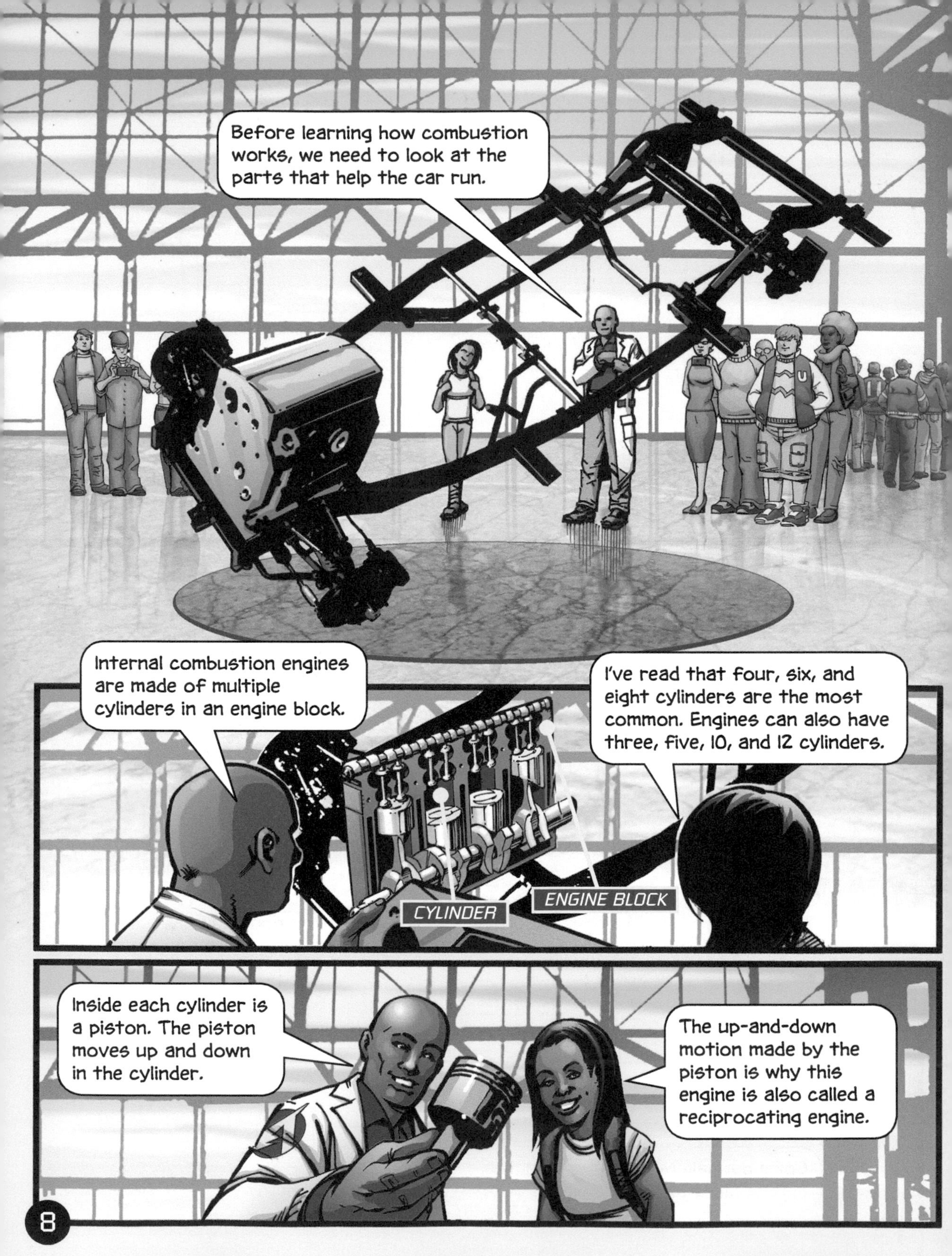
Before learning how combustion works, we need to look at the parts that help the car run.
Internal combustion engines are made of multiple cylinders in an engine block.
I've read that four, six, and eight cylinders are the most common. Engines can also have three, five, 10, and 12 cylinders.
CYLINDER
ENGINE BLOCK
Inside each cylinder is a piston. The piston moves up and down in the cylinder.
The up-and-down motion made by the piston is why this engine is also called a reciprocating engine.

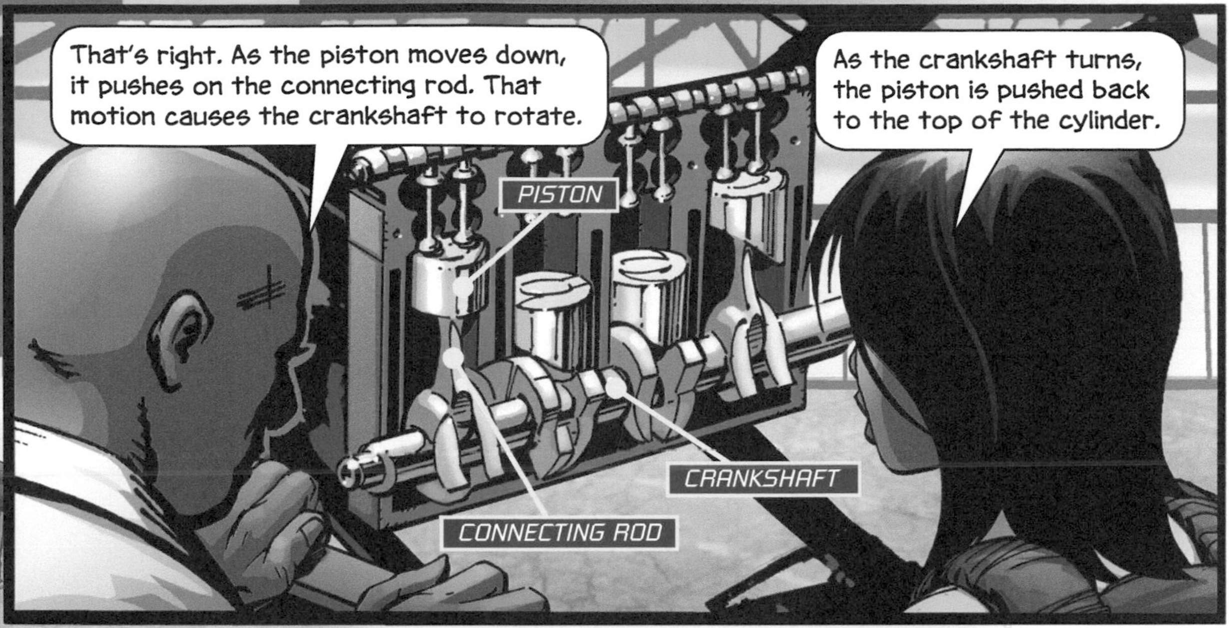
That's right. As the piston moves down, it pushes on the connecting rod. That motion causes the crankshaft to rotate.
As the crankshaft turns, the piston is pushed back to the top of the cylinder.
PISTON
CRANKSHAFT
CONNECTING ROD

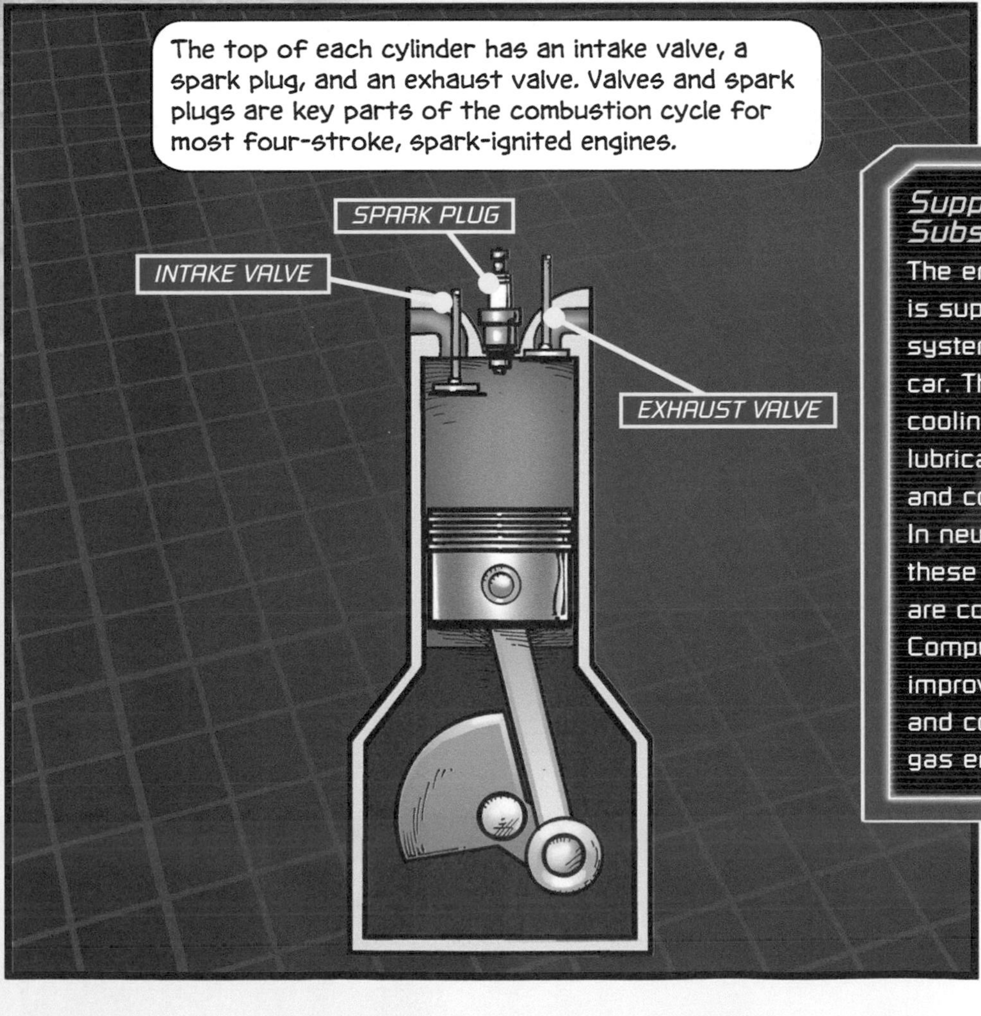
The top of each cylinder has an intake valve, a spark plug, and an exhaust valve. Valves and spark plugs are key parts of the combustion cycle for most four-stroke, spark-ignited engines.
SPARK PLUG
INTAKE VALVE
EXHAUST VALVE

Supportive Subsystems

The engine system is supported by other systems within the car. They include the cooling, fuel delivery, lubrication, electrical, and control systems. In newer cars, all these systems are computerized. Computers help improve fuel economy and control exhaust gas emissions.

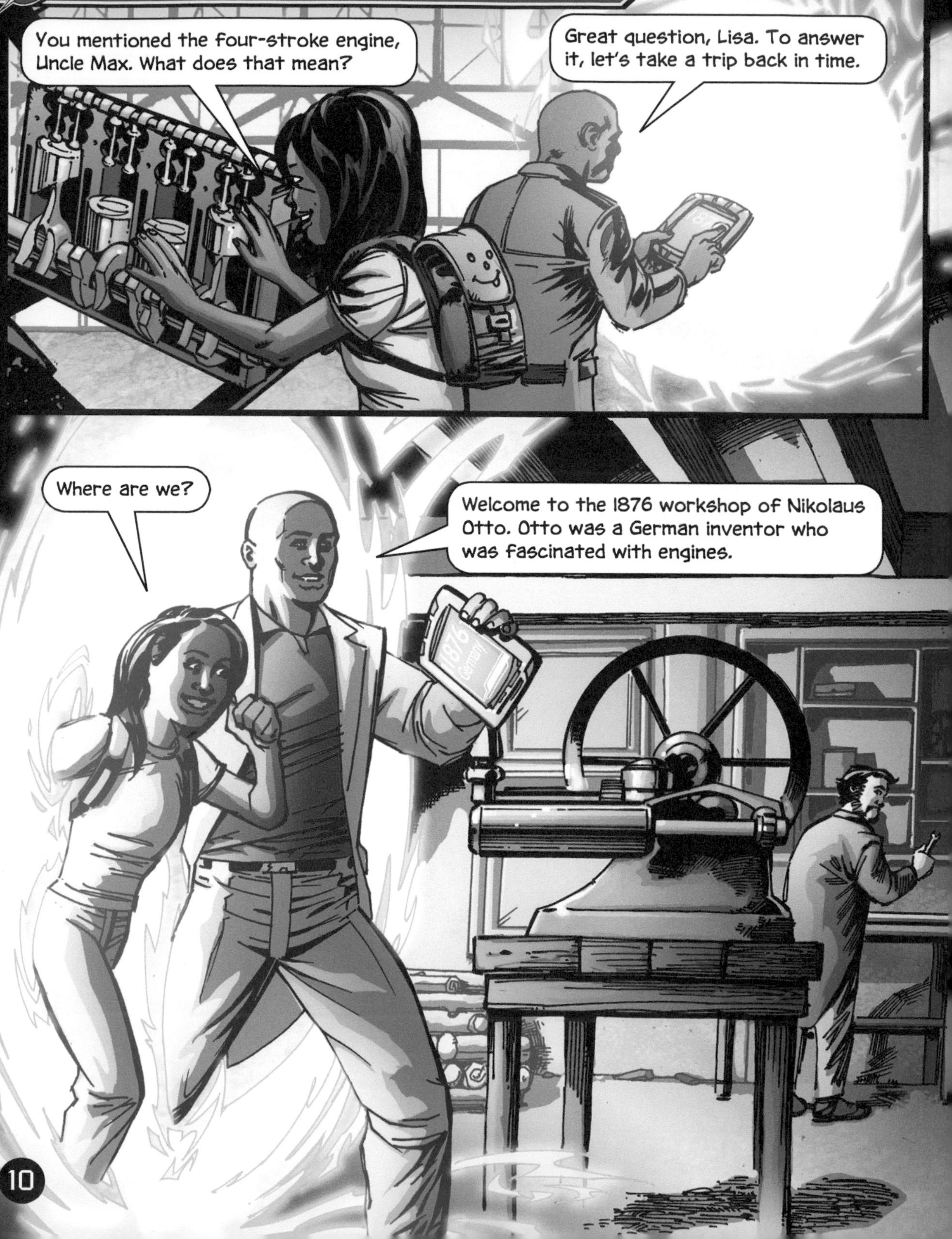
You mentioned the four-stroke engine, Uncle Max. What does that mean?
Great question, Lisa. To answer it, let's take a trip back in time.
Where are we?
Welcome to the 1876 workshop of Nikolaus Otto. Otto was a German inventor who was fascinated with engines.
1876
Germany

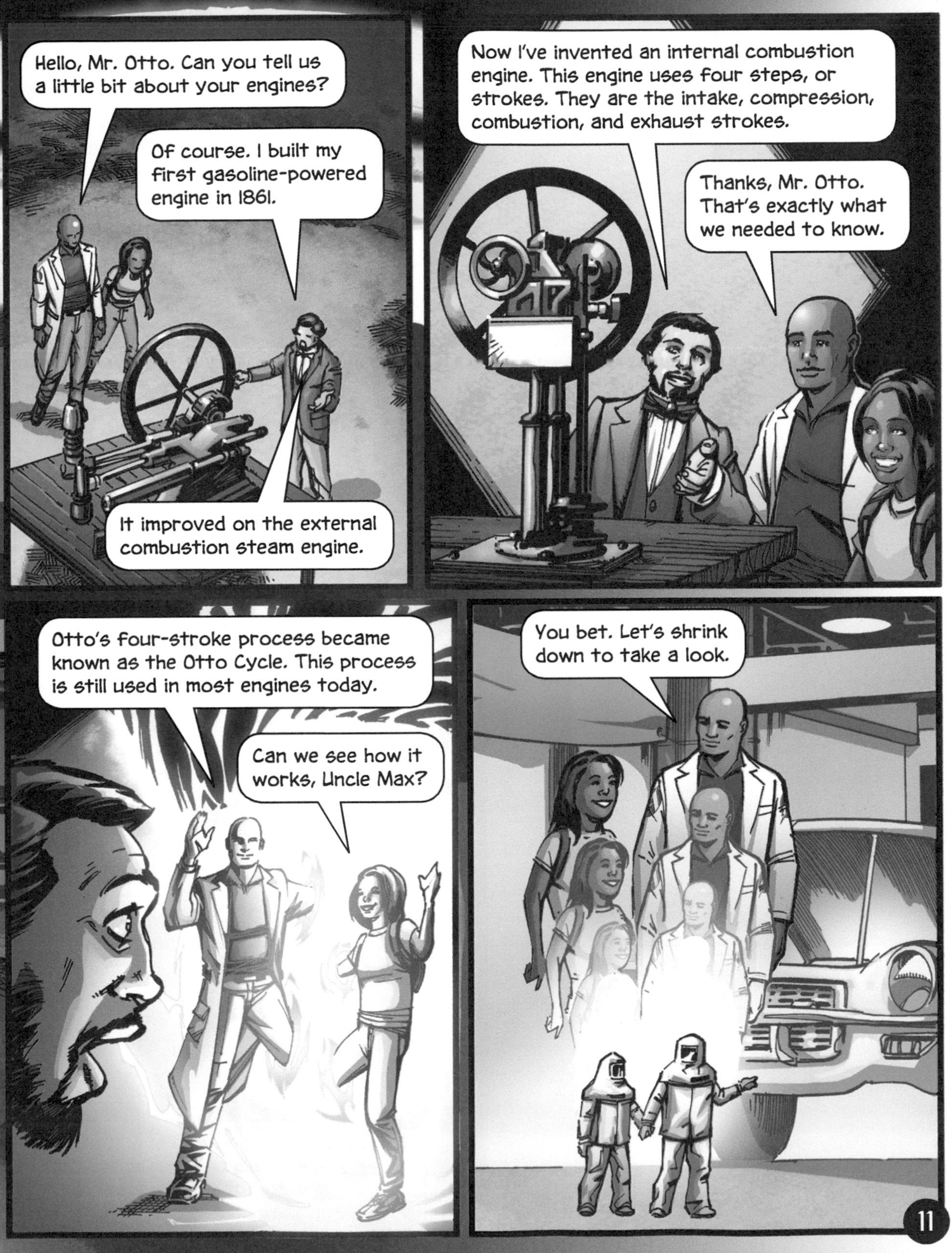
Hello, Mr. Otto. Can you tell us a little bit about your engines?
Of course. I built my first gasoline-powered engine in 1861.
It improved on the external combustion steam engine.
Now I've invented an internal combustion engine. This engine uses four steps, or strokes. They are the intake, compression, combustion, and exhaust strokes.
Thanks, Mr. Otto. That's exactly what we needed to know.
Otto's four-stroke process became known as the Otto Cycle. This process is still used in most engines today.
Can we see how it works, Uncle Max?
You bet. Let's shrink down to take a look.

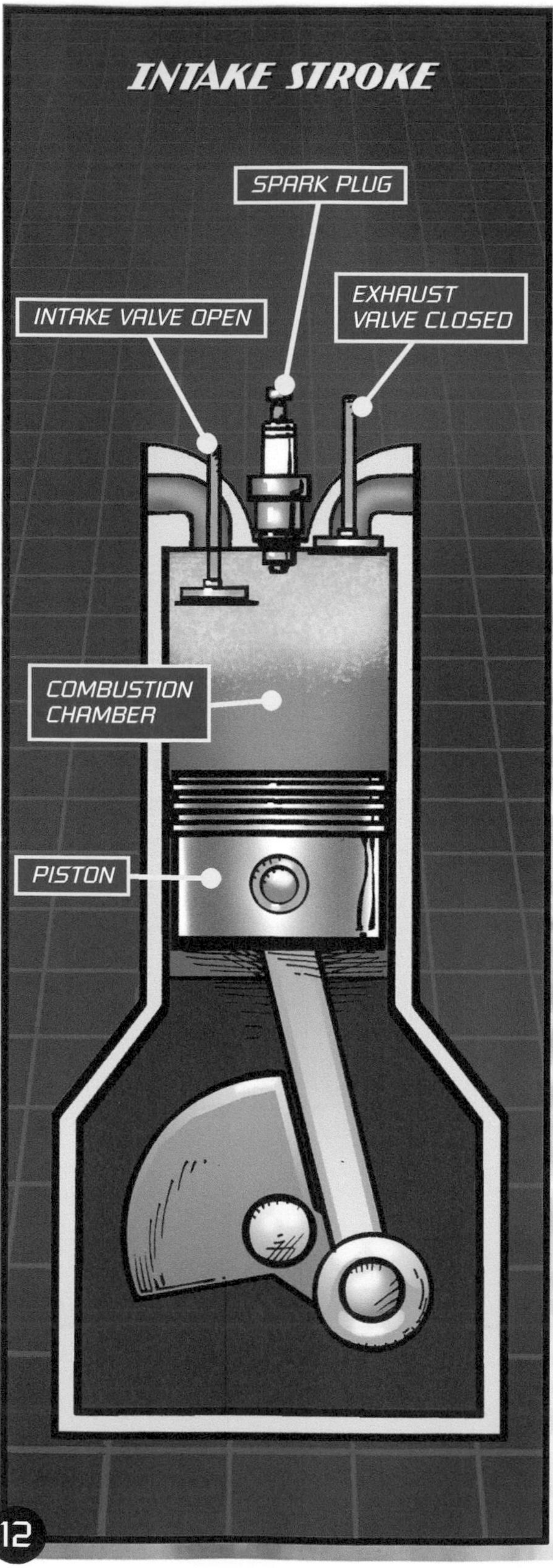
INTAKE STROKE
SPARK PLUG
INTAKE VALVE OPEN
EXHAUST VALVE CLOSED
COMBUSTION CHAMBER
PISTON

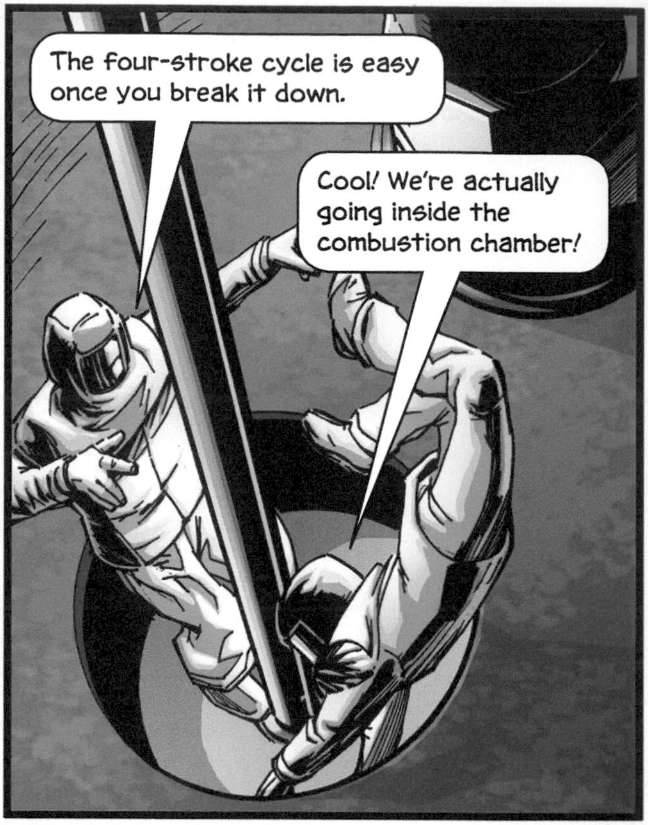
The four-stroke cycle is easy once you break it down.
Cool! We're actually going inside the combustion chamber!

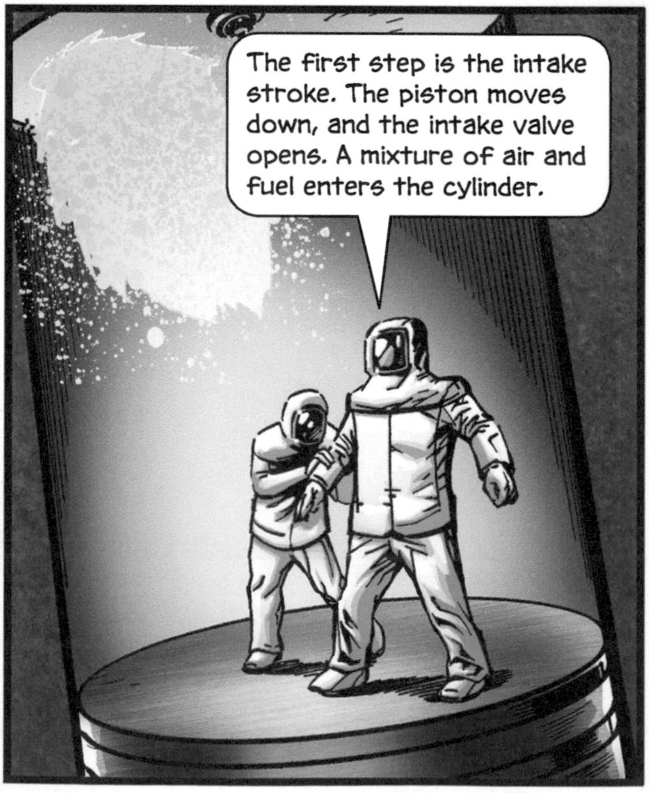
The first step is the intake stroke. The piston moves down, and the intake valve opens. A mixture of air and fuel enters the cylinder.

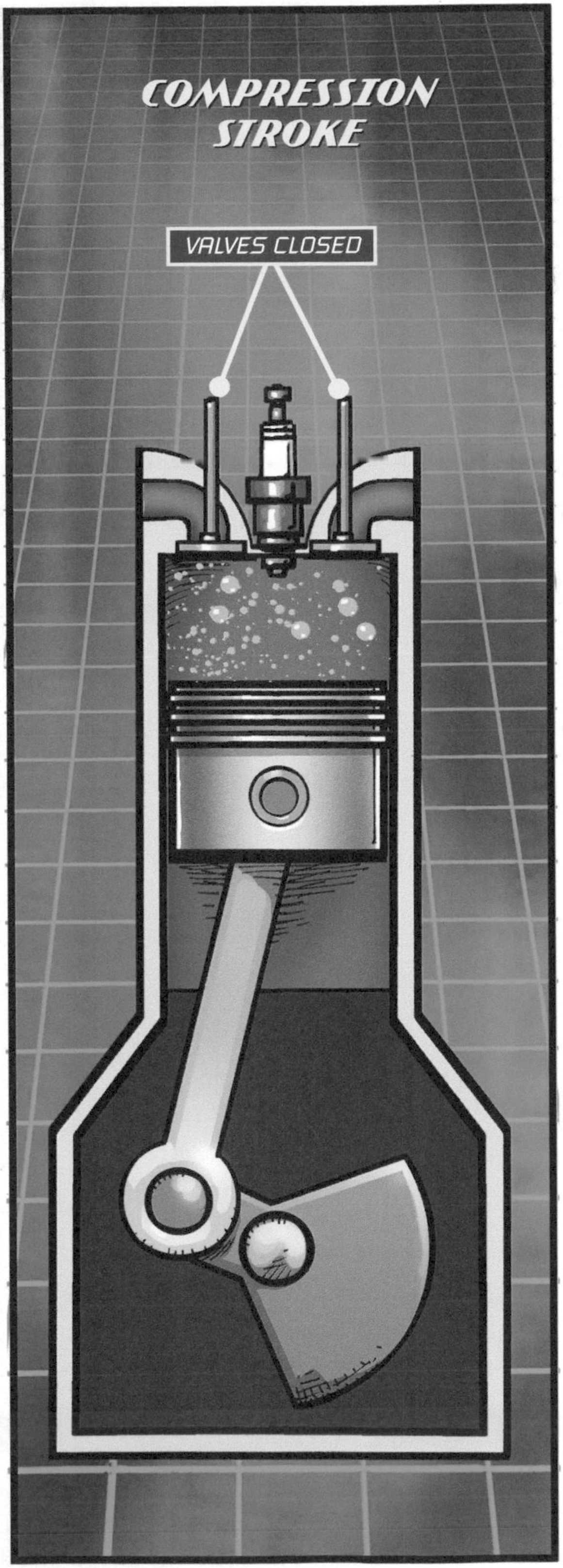
COMPRESSION STROKE
VALVES CLOSED

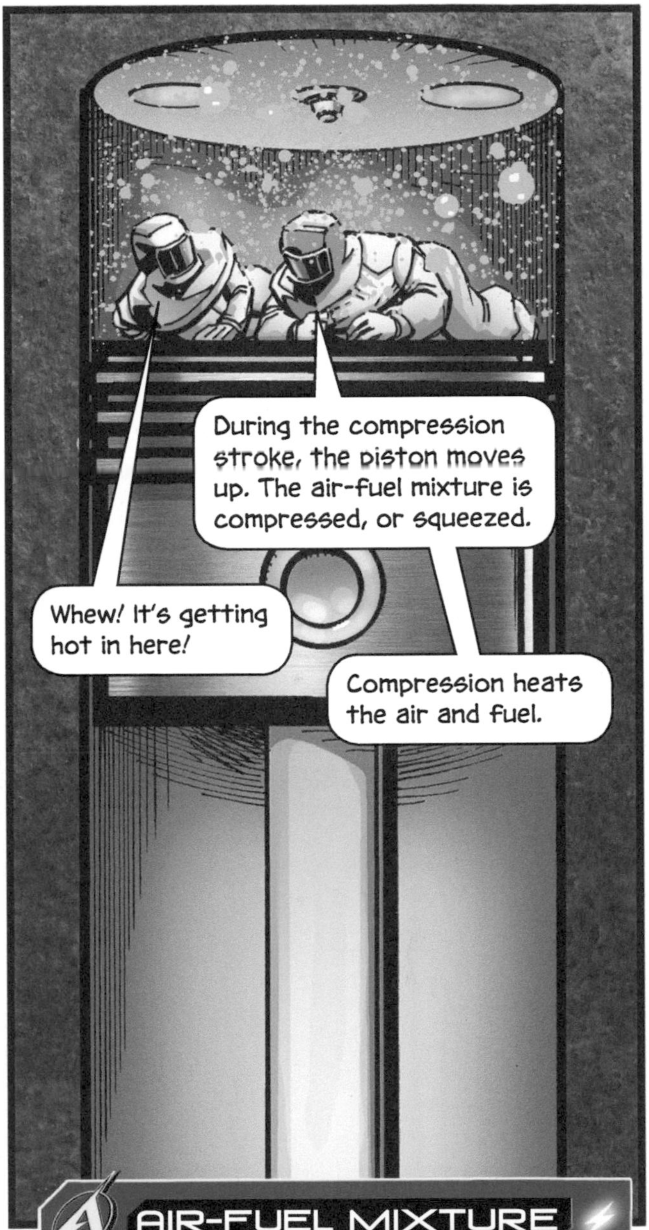
During the compression stroke, the piston moves up. The air-fuel mixture is compressed, or squeezed.
Whew! It's getting hot in here!
Compression heats the air and fuel.

AIR-FUEL MIXTURE

The air-fuel mixture uses a lot more air than gasoline. It is made up of about 15 parts of air to one part gasoline. During combustion, about 10,000 gallons (37,850 liters) of air is used for every gallon of fuel.

COMBUSTION STROKE

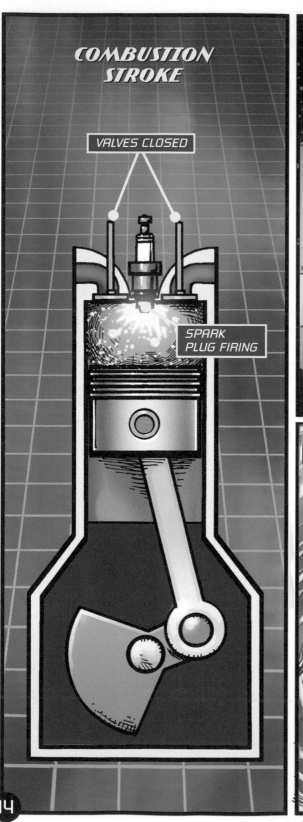

VALVES CLOSED

SPARK PLUG FIRING

When the piston reaches the top of the stroke, the spark plug fires. The heated air-fuel mixture allows the spark to create flames.

These flames race across the cylinder and the hot gases expand rapidly.

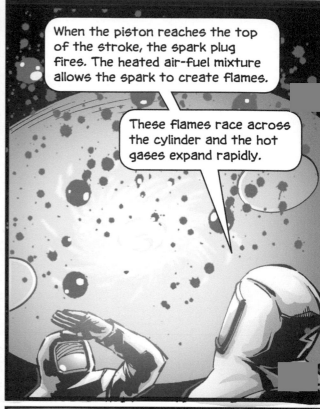

The rapidly expanding gases drive the piston to the bottom of the combustion chamber.

WHEEE!!!

EXHAUST STROKE

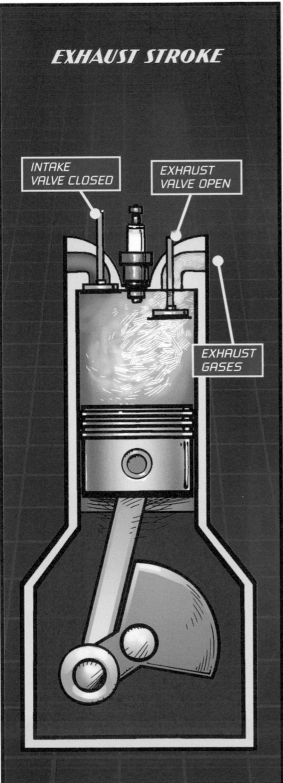

INTAKE VALVE CLOSED

EXHAUST VALVE OPEN

EXHAUST GASES

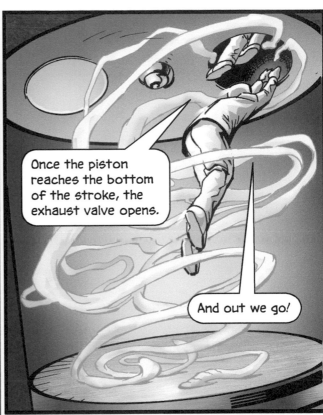

Once the piston reaches the bottom of the stroke, the exhaust valve opens.

And out we go!

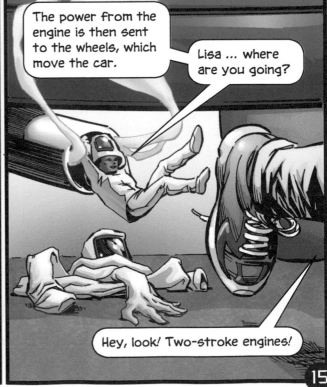

The power from the engine is then sent to the wheels, which move the car.

Lisa ... where are you going?

Hey, look! Two-stroke engines!

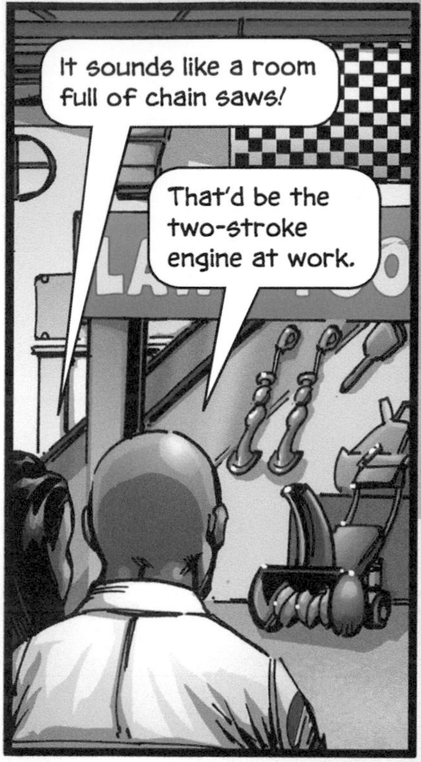
It sounds like a room full of chain saws!
That'd be the two-stroke engine at work.

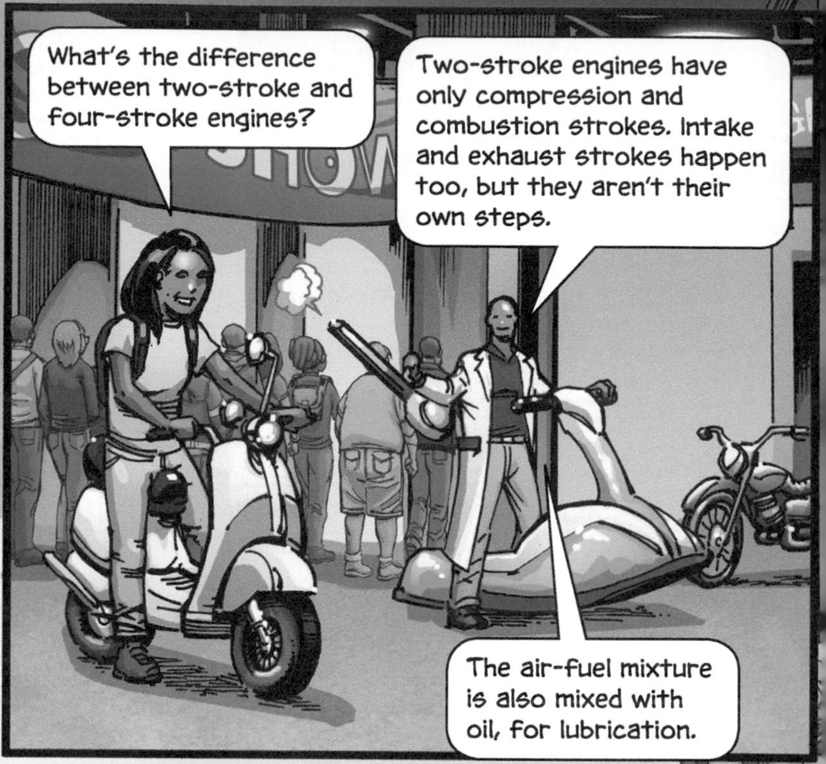
What's the difference between two-stroke and four-stroke engines?
Two-stroke engines have only compression and combustion strokes. Intake and exhaust strokes happen too, but they aren't their own steps.
The air-fuel mixture is also mixed with oil, for lubrication.

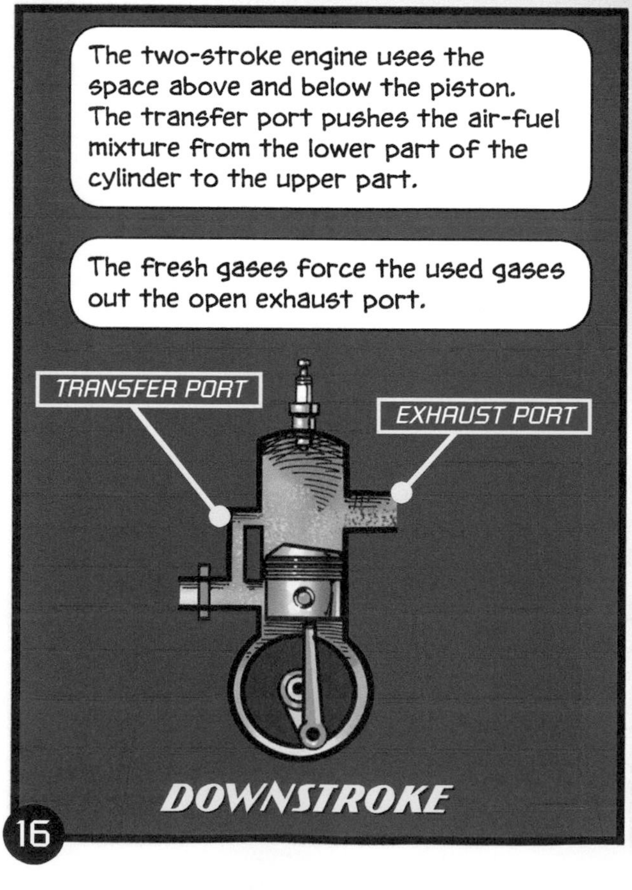
The two-stroke engine uses the space above and below the piston. The transfer port pushes the air-fuel mixture from the lower part of the cylinder to the upper part.
The fresh gases force the used gases out the open exhaust port.
TRANSFER PORT
EXHAUST PORT
DOWNSTROKE

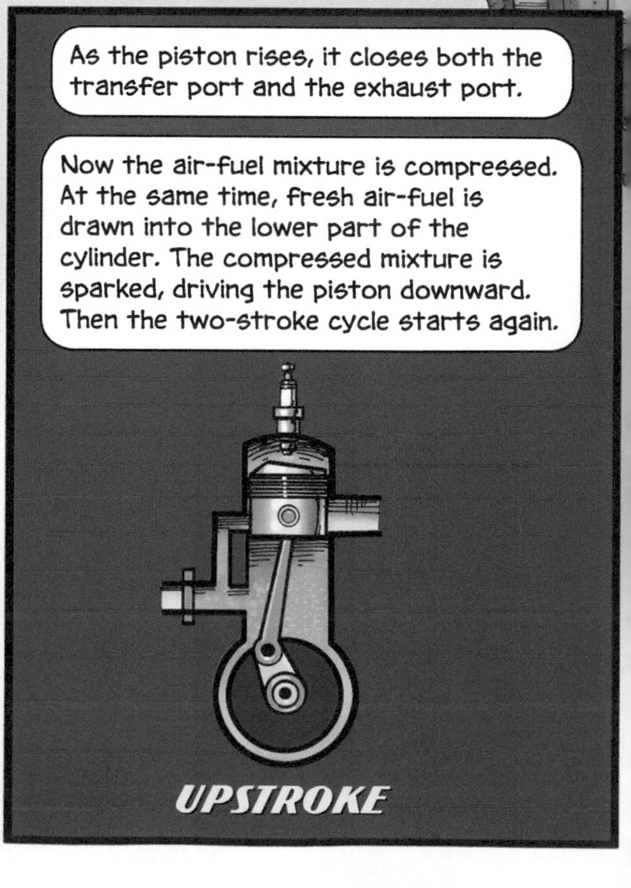
As the piston rises, it closes both the transfer port and the exhaust port.
Now the air-fuel mixture is compressed. At the same time, fresh air-fuel is drawn into the lower part of the cylinder. The compressed mixture is sparked, driving the piston downward. Then the two-stroke cycle starts again.
UPSTROKE

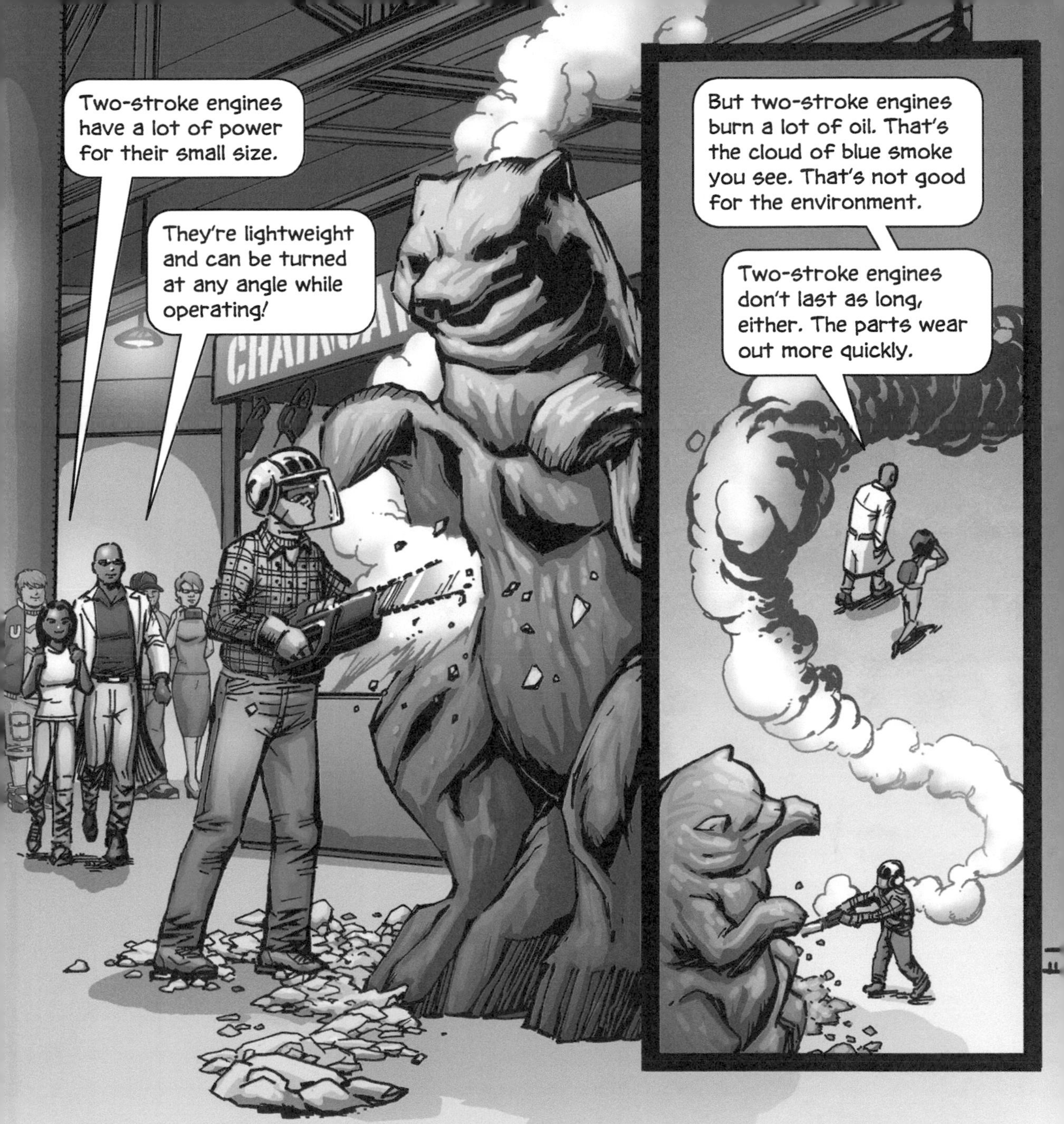
Two-stroke engines have a lot of power for their small size.
They're lightweight and can be turned at any angle while operating!
But two-stroke engines burn a lot of oil. That's the cloud of blue smoke you see. That's not good for the environment.
Two-stroke engines don't last as long, either. The parts wear out more quickly.

BURNING OIL

Two-stroke engines use 4 ounces (118 milliliters) of oil per gallon of gas. If a car engine worked the same way, 1 gallon (3.8 liters) of oil would be burned every 1,000 miles (1,600 kilometers). The average American driver would create a lot more pollution by burning through more than 13 gallons (49 liters) of oil every year.

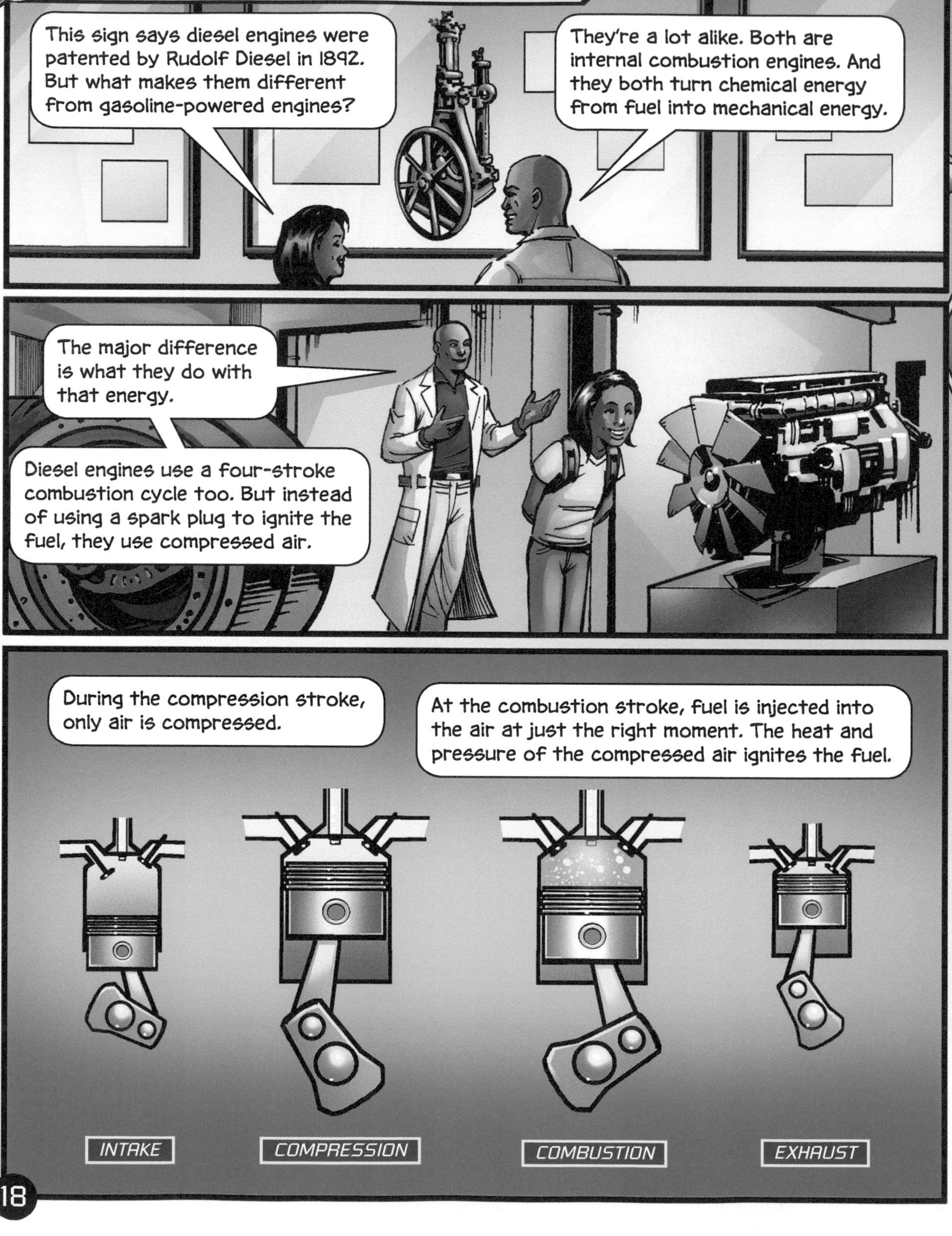
This sign says diesel engines were patented by Rudolf Diesel in 1892. But what makes them different from gasoline-powered engines?
They're a lot alike. Both are internal combustion engines. And they both turn chemical energy from fuel into mechanical energy.
The major difference is what they do with that energy.
Diesel engines use a four-stroke combustion cycle too. But instead of using a spark plug to ignite the fuel, they use compressed air.
During the compression stroke, only air is compressed.
At the combustion stroke, fuel is injected into the air at just the right moment. The heat and pressure of the compressed air ignites the fuel.
INTAKE
COMPRESSION
COMBUSTION
EXHAUST

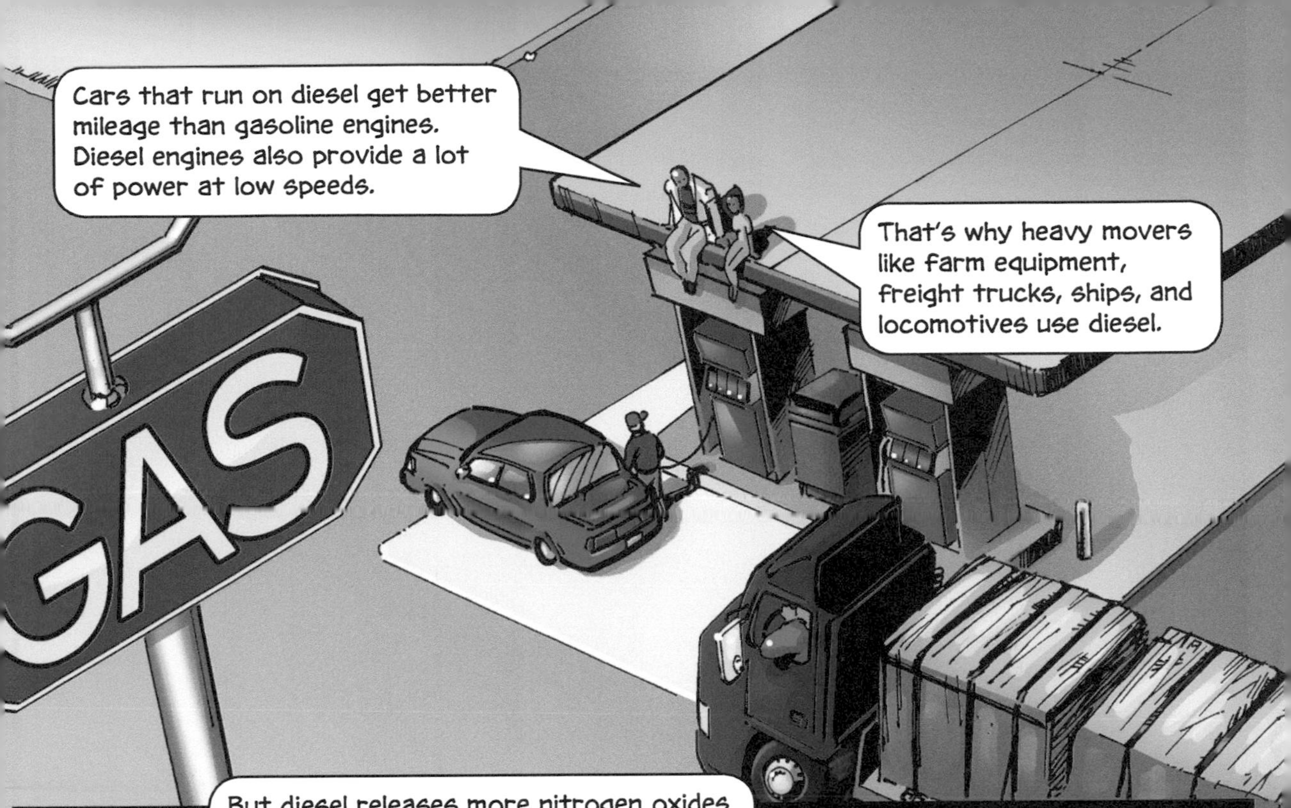
Cars that run on diesel get better mileage than gasoline engines. Diesel engines also provide a lot of power at low speeds.
That's why heavy movers like farm equipment, freight trucks, ships, and locomotives use diesel.
GAS

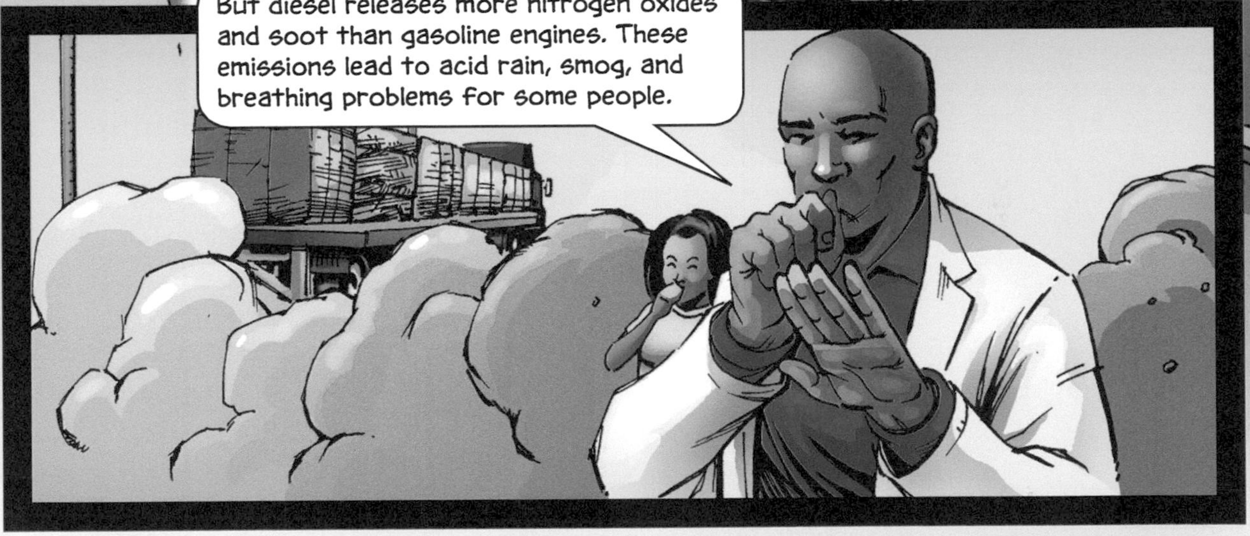
But diesel releases more nitrogen oxides and soot than gasoline engines. These emissions lead to acid rain, smog, and breathing problems for some people.

BIODIESEL

ACCESS GRANTED: MAX AXIOM

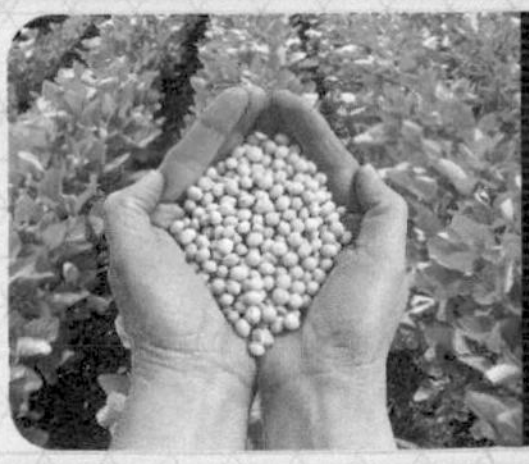

Biodiesel is an alternative fuel made from plant oils or animal fats. It usually produces less soot than diesel made from fossil fuels. It's also biodegradable. Biodiesel made from plant matter also helps reduce greenhouse gases released by engines. Biodiesel can be used by itself or blended with regular diesel.

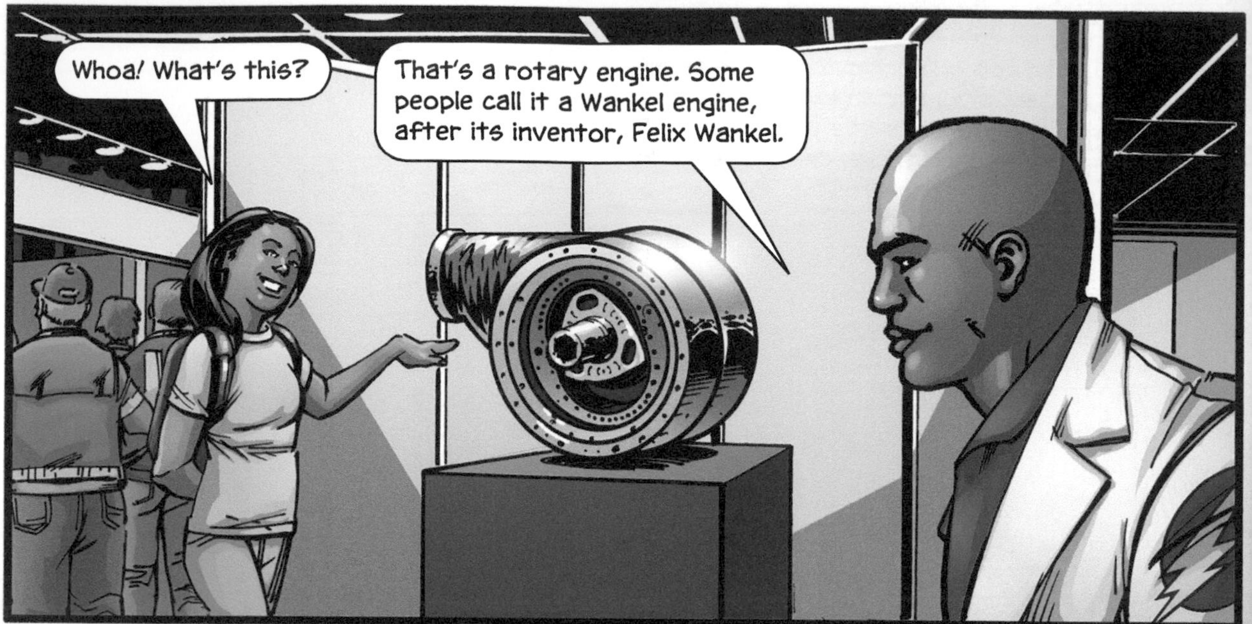
Whoa! What's this?
That's a rotary engine. Some people call it a Wankel engine, after its inventor, Felix Wankel.

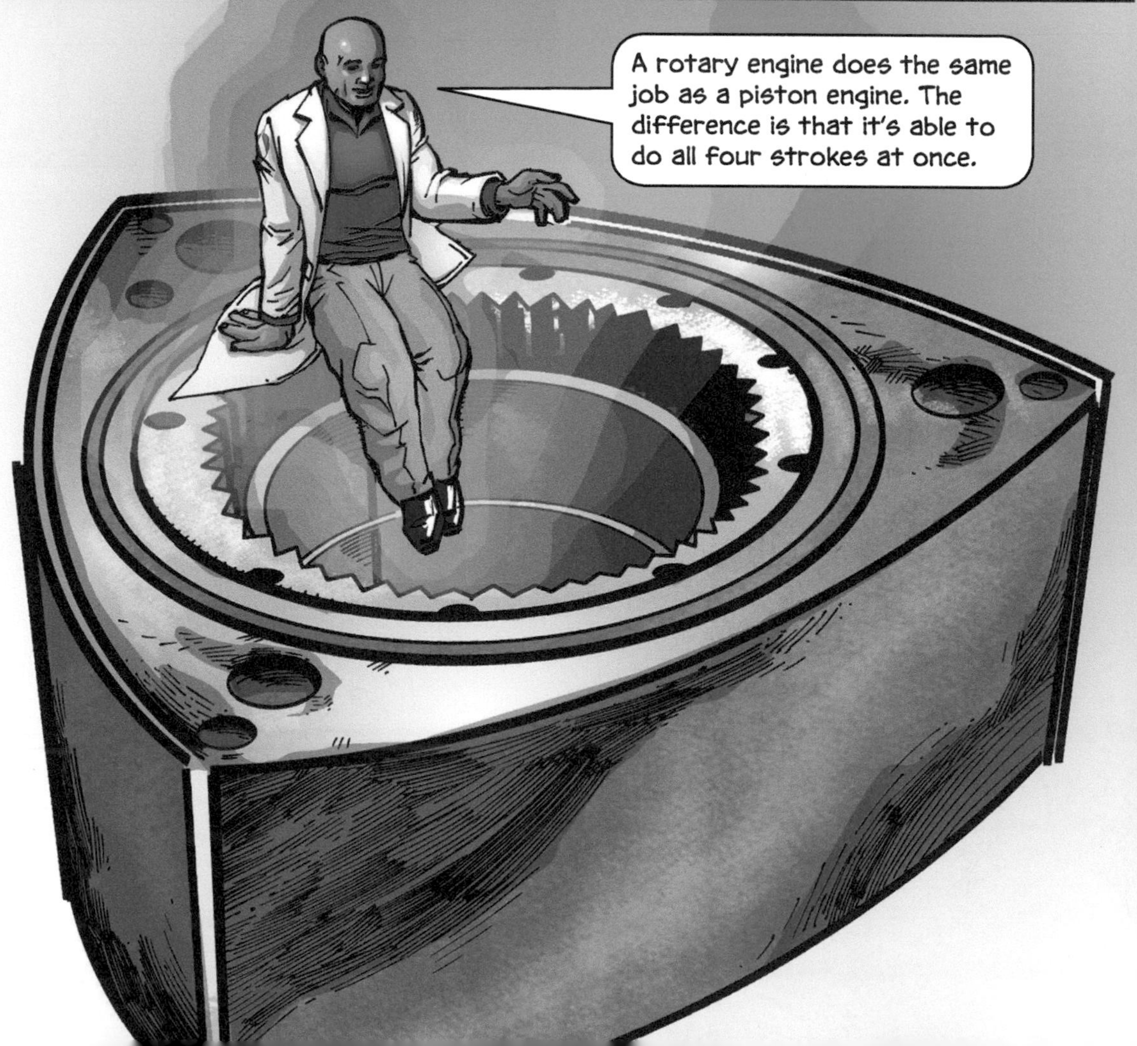
A rotary engine does the same job as a piston engine. The difference is that it's able to do all four strokes at once.

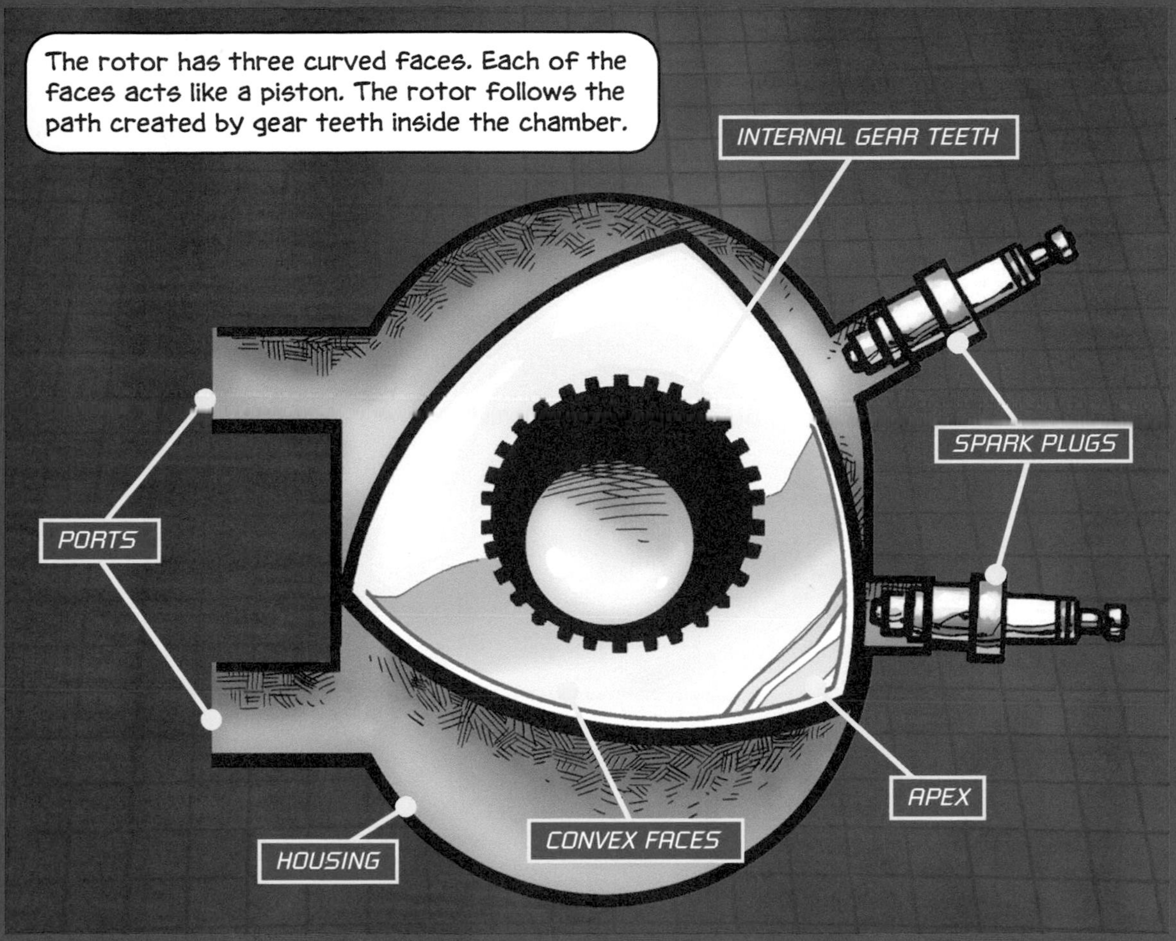
The rotor has three curved faces. Each of the faces acts like a piston. The rotor follows the path created by gear teeth inside the chamber.
INTERNAL GEAR TEETH
SPARK PLUGS
PORTS
APEX
CONVEX FACES
HOUSING

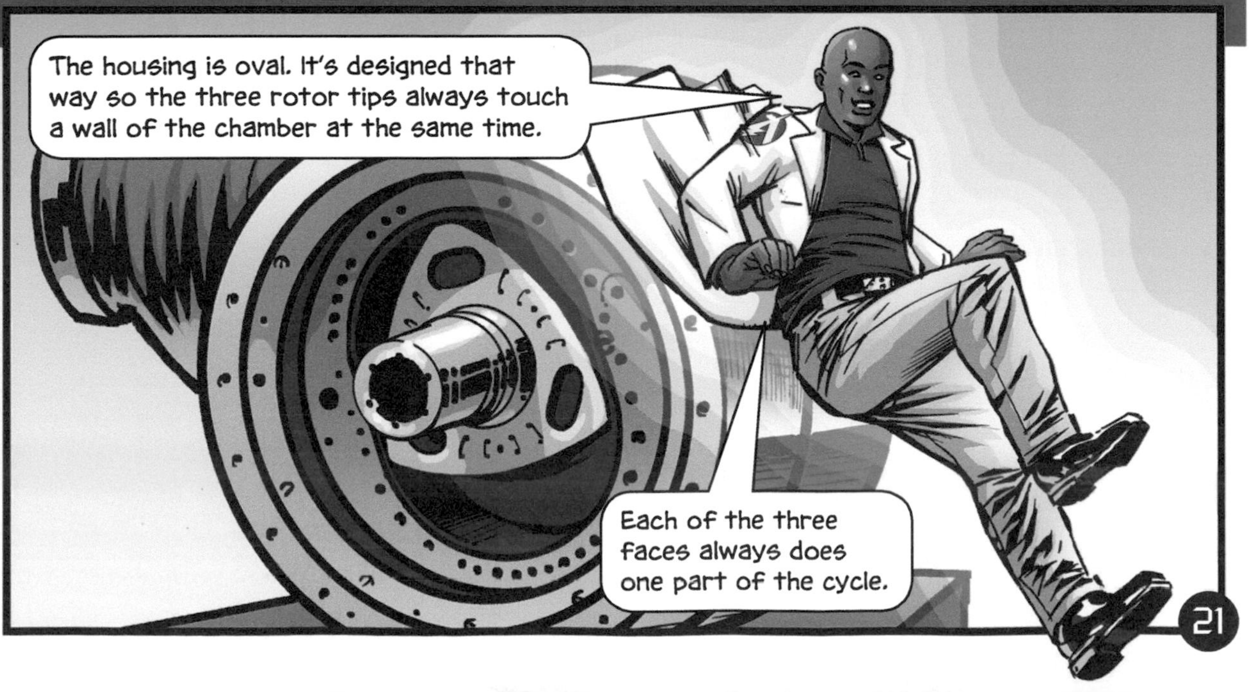
The housing is oval. It's designed that way so the three rotor tips always touch a wall of the chamber at the same time.
Each of the three faces always does one part of the cycle.

Before the intake stroke, the volume of that chamber is at its smallest. As the rotor moves past the intake port, the chamber expands, drawing air-fuel in. When the peak of the rotor moves past the port, the chamber is sealed.

INTAKE

As the rotor continues its motion, the chamber gets smaller. This motion compresses the air-fuel mixture. By the time the rotor reaches the spark plugs, the chamber is again at its smallest.

COMPRESSION

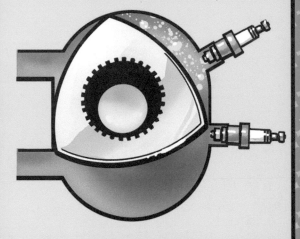

Rotary engines have two spark plugs. These plugs ensure the flame spreads quickly. The air-fuel mixture ignites, keeping the rotor moving.

COMBUSTION

SPARK PLUGS

The rotor continues to move, compressing the chamber. The spent gases go out the exhaust port. When the rotor reaches the intake port, the cycle starts again.

EXHAUST

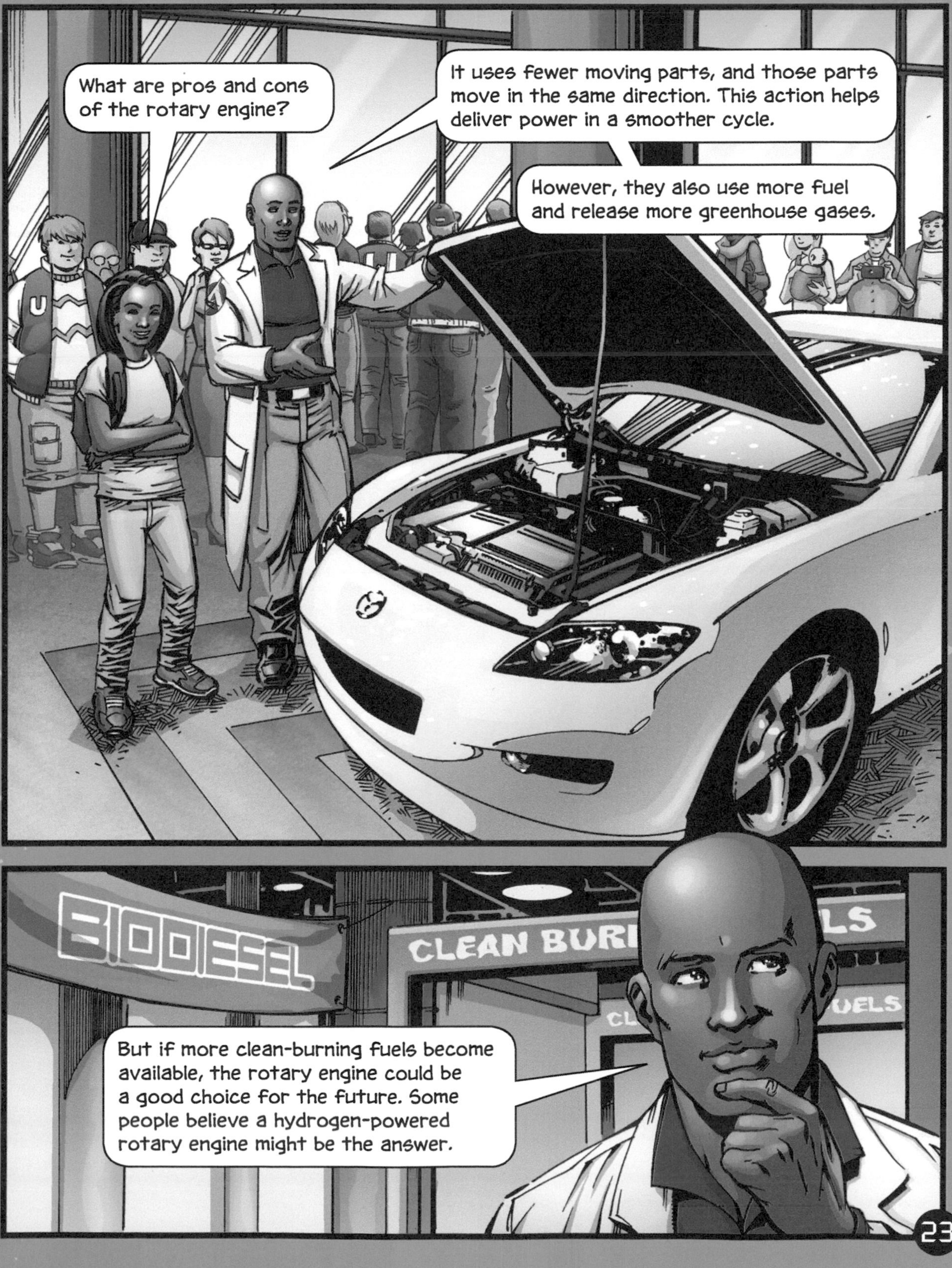
What are pros and cons of the rotary engine?
It uses fewer moving parts, and those parts move in the same direction. This action helps deliver power in a smoother cycle.
However, they also use more fuel and release more greenhouse gases.
BIODIESEL
CLEAN BUR
LS
But if more clean-burning fuels become available, the rotary engine could be a good choice for the future. Some people believe a hydrogen-powered rotary engine might be the answer.

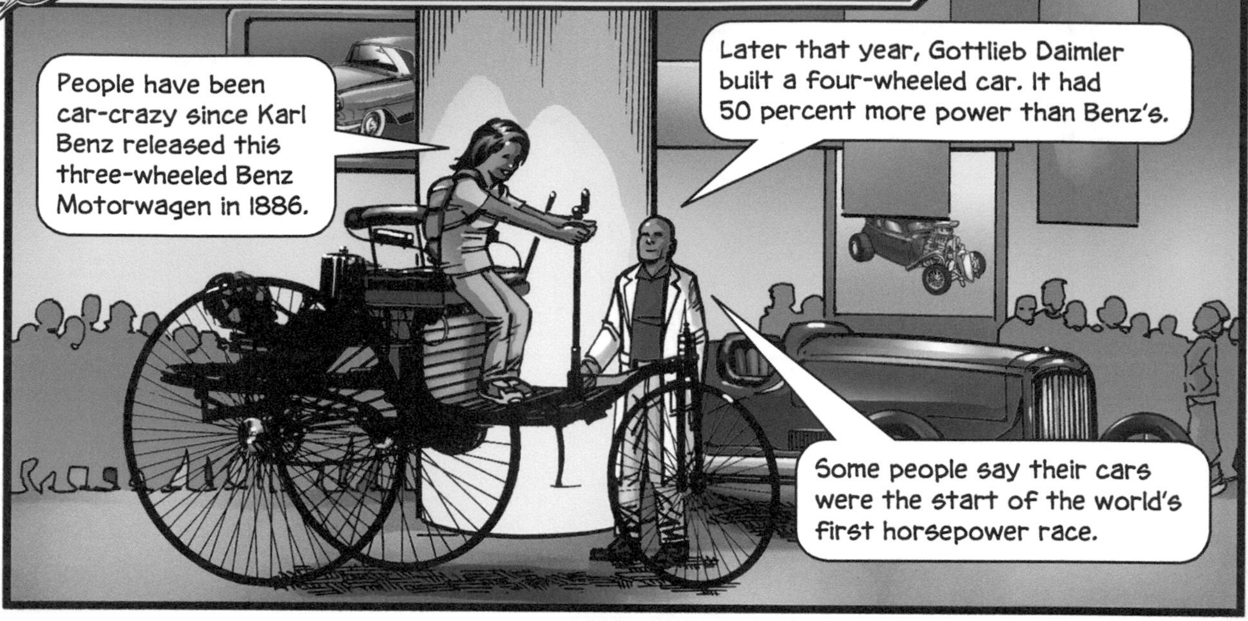
People have been car-crazy since Karl Benz released this three-wheeled Benz Motorwagen in 1886.
Later that year, Gottlieb Daimler built a four-wheeled car. It had 50 percent more power than Benz's.
Some people say their cars were the start of the world's first horsepower race.

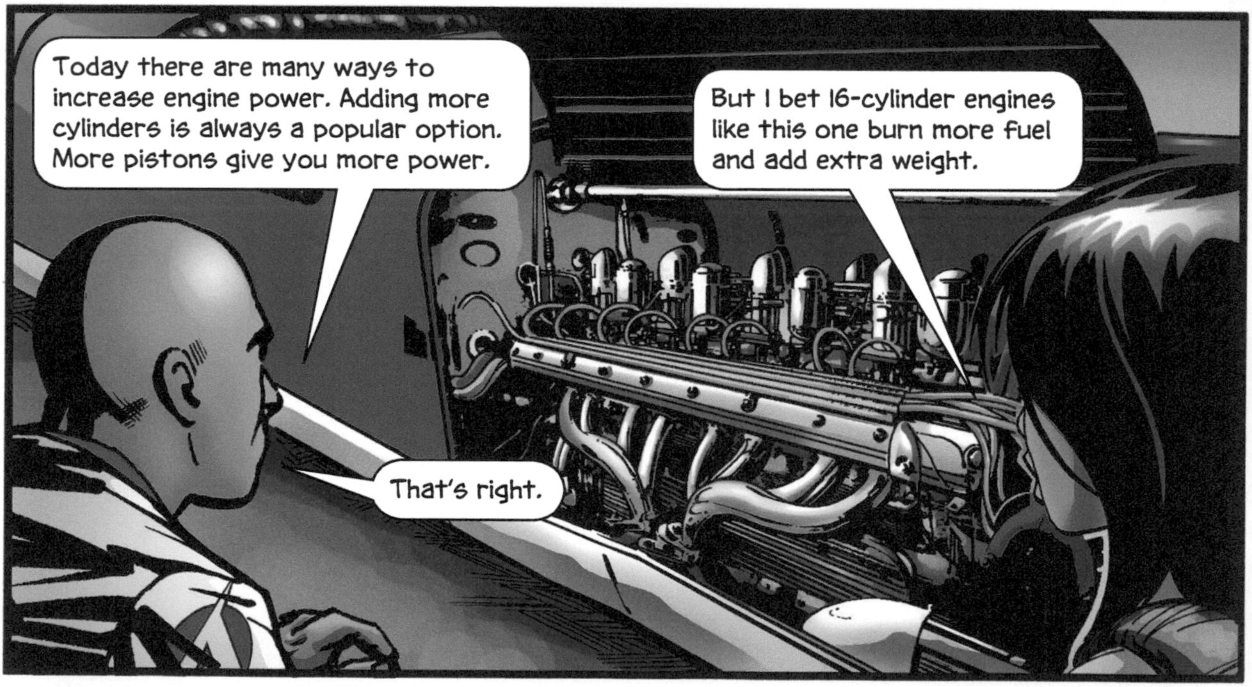
Today there are many ways to increase engine power. Adding more cylinders is always a popular option. More pistons give you more power.
But I bet 16-cylinder engines like this one burn more fuel and add extra weight.
That's right.

MOVING BY HORSEPOWER

Horsepower is the measurement of an engine's ability to do work. One horsepower equals the amount of work it would take to lift 550 pounds (250 kilograms) 1 foot (31 centimeters) in one second.

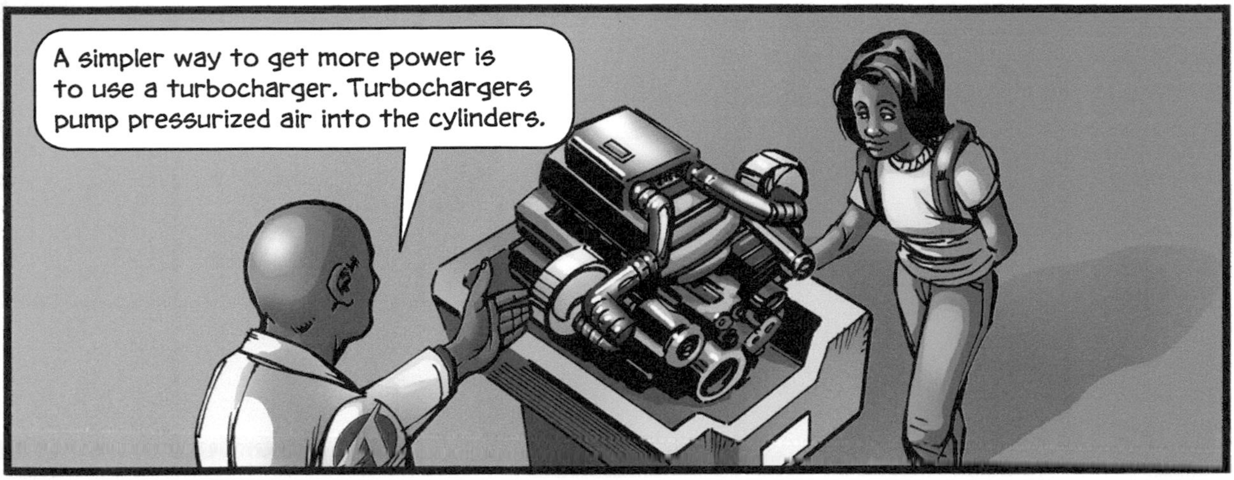
A simpler way to get more power is to use a turbocharger. Turbochargers pump pressurized air into the cylinders.

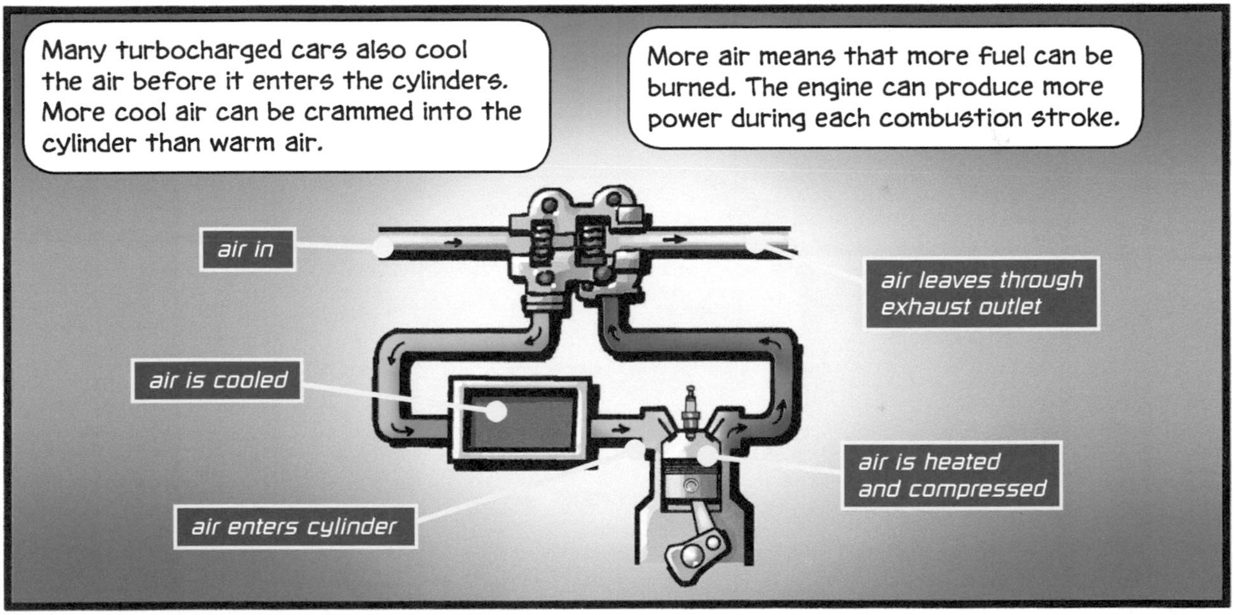
Many turbocharged cars also cool the air before it enters the cylinders. More cool air can be crammed into the cylinder than warm air.
More air means that more fuel can be burned. The engine can produce more power during each combustion stroke.
air in
air leaves through exhaust outlet
air is cooled
air is heated and compressed
air enters cylinder

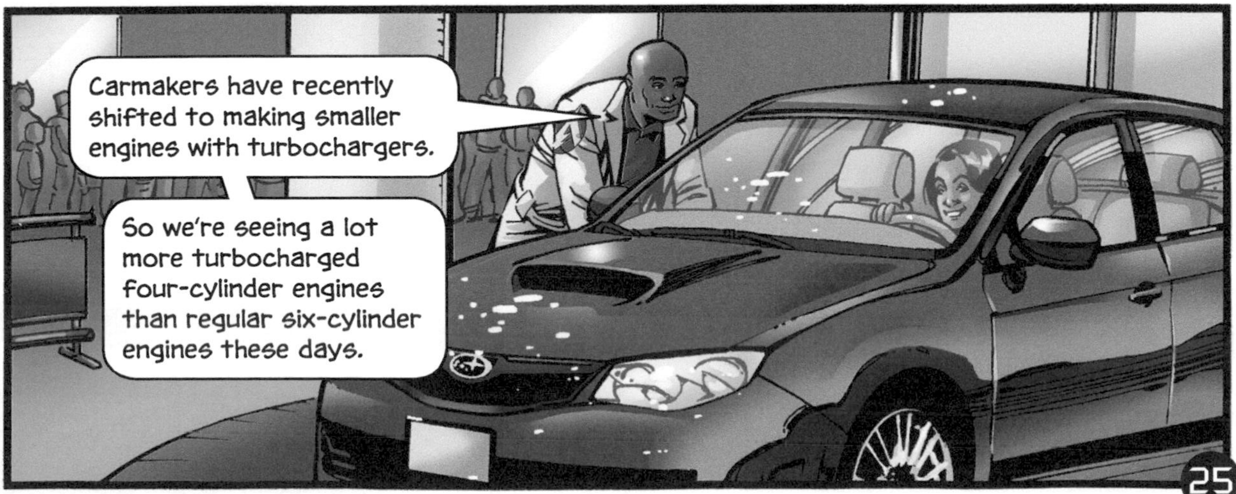
Carmakers have recently shifted to making smaller engines with turbochargers.
So we're seeing a lot more turbocharged four-cylinder engines than regular six-cylinder engines these days.

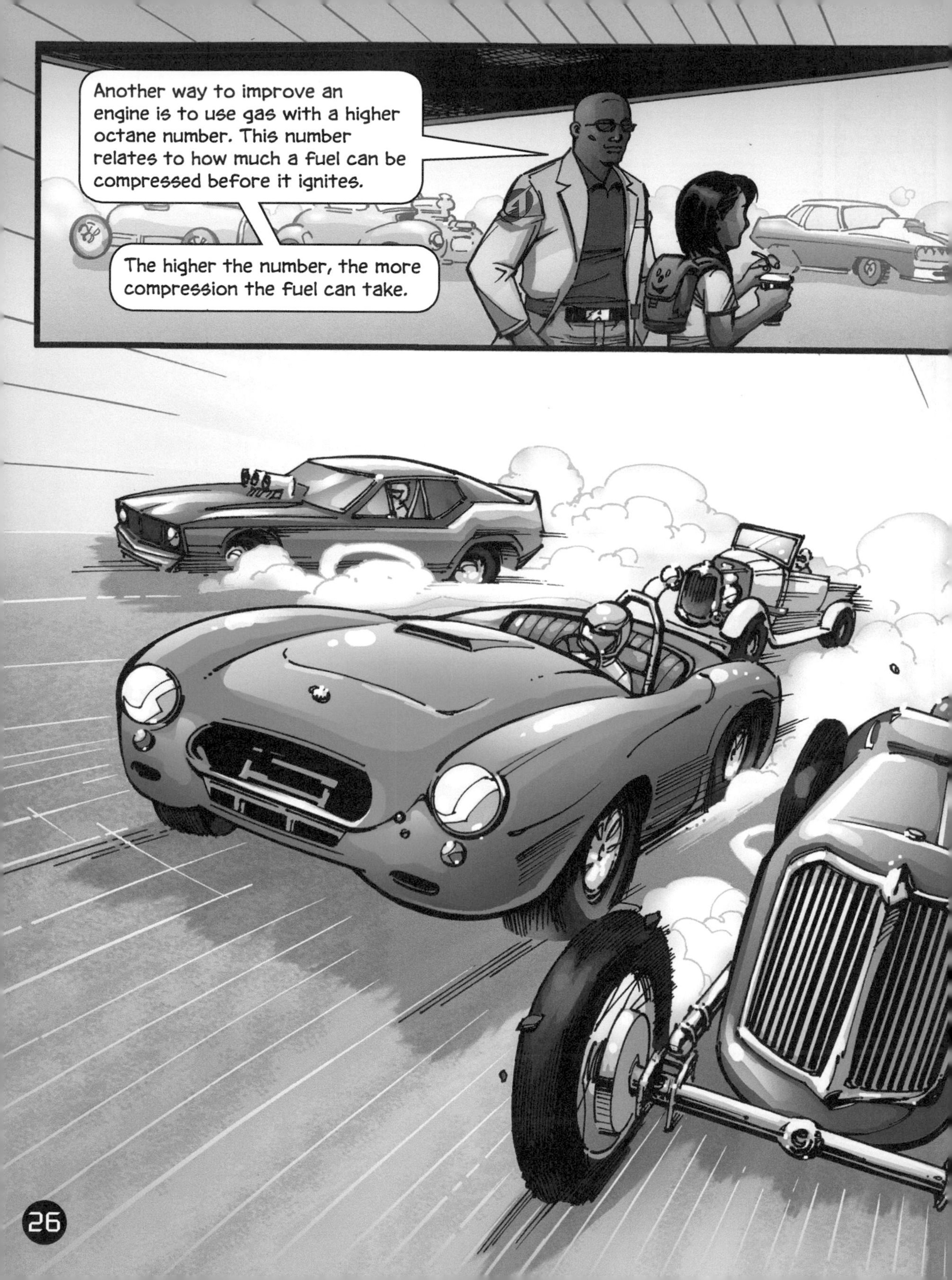
Another way to improve an engine is to use gas with a higher octane number. This number relates to how much a fuel can be compressed before it ignites.
The higher the number, the more compression the fuel can take.

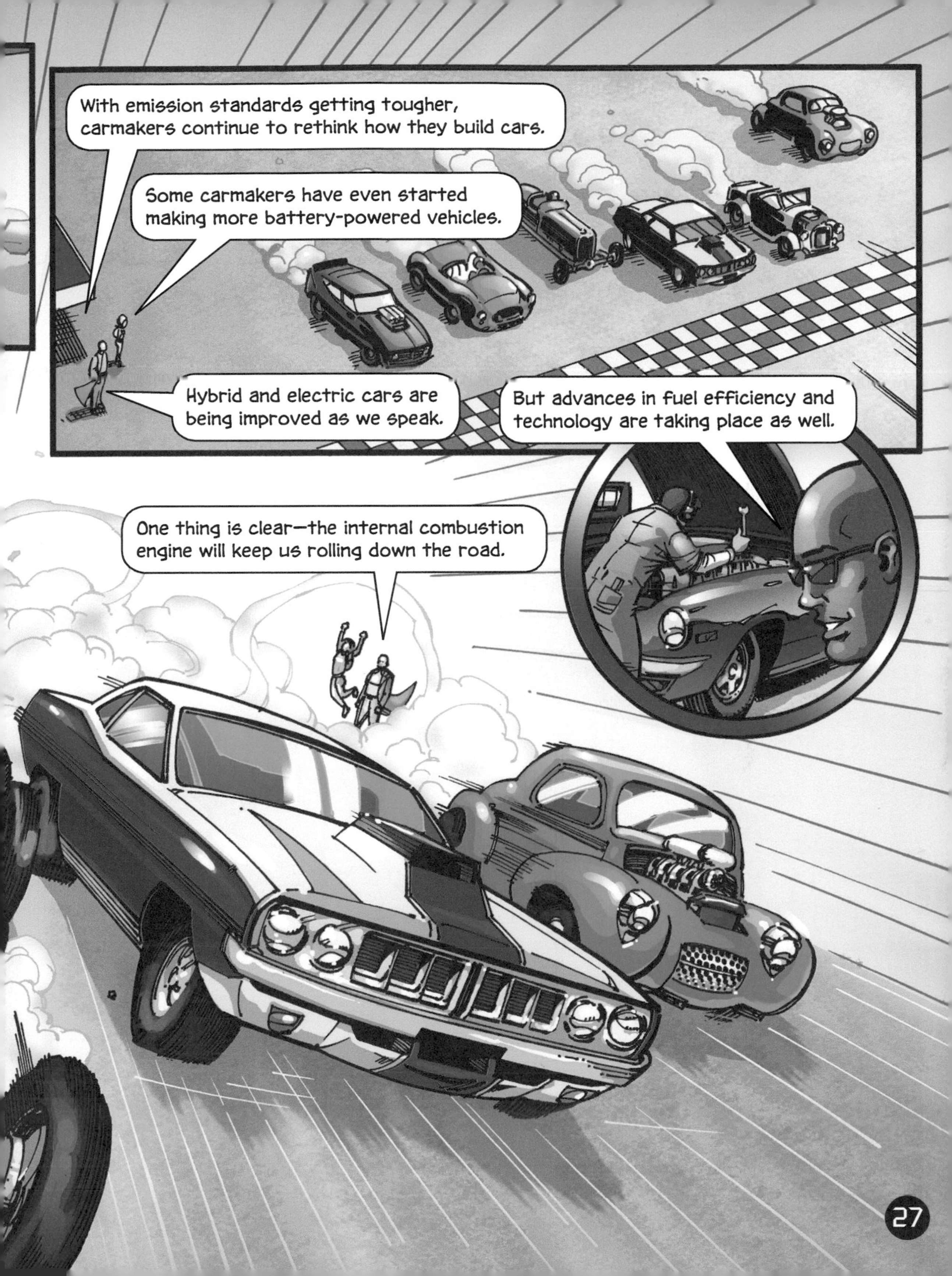
With emission standards getting tougher, carmakers continue to rethink how they build cars.
Some carmakers have even started making more battery-powered vehicles.
Hybrid and electric cars are being improved as we speak.
But advances in fuel efficiency and technology are taking place as well.
One thing is clear—the internal combustion engine will keep us rolling down the road.

MORE ABOUT THE
INTERNAL COMBUSTION ENGINE

The first general-use internal combustion engine was built by Étienne Lenoir in 1860. It was a two-stroke engine that used a mixture of coal gas and air.

Most car engines add fuel into the cylinder during the intake stroke. Then the fuel is compressed. Normally only the spark should ignite the air-fuel mixture. But if the air is compressed too much, the mixture ignites spontaneously. This explosion causes a loud noise known as knocking. Knocking creates extra heat and can damage the engine.

Gasoline and diesel are called fossil fuels. They are made from oil formed by plants and animals that lived millions of years ago. Biofuels and biodiesel are made from plants and animals living today. In 2012 the United States produced more than 960 million gallons (3.6 billion liters) of biodiesel.

Gasoline gives you a lot of energy for a small amount of fuel. An average car can travel 400 miles (644 km) on a single tank of gasoline. An electric car would have to be recharged at least once over the same distance. A hydrogen car would need a huge fuel tank or be able to compress the hydrogen to very high pressures. Even biofuel wouldn't get you quite as far as gasoline if you used the same volume fuel tank.

Hybrid cars use power from both an engine and an electric motor. The motor takes some of the demand off the engine, which means less gas is used. However, hybrids require complex and expensive technology to control the engine and motor together.

CRITICAL THINKING USING THE COMMON CORE

1. On pages 10 and 11, the author shows Max and Lisa traveling back to the past. Why do you think the author wrote the scene this way? How does it help your understanding of the internal combustion engine? (Craft and Structure)

2. On page 17, a man uses a chain saw as Max and Lisa explain two-stroke engines. Make a list of other tools or vehicles you think might use two-stroke engines. Why would these items benefit from a two-stroke instead of a four-stroke engine? (Integration of Knowledge and Ideas)

3. Why is air such an important part of the combustion cycle? Explain how turbochargers use air and why they give engines more power. (Key Ideas and Details)

MORE ABOUT

SUPER SCIENTIST

Real name: Maxwell J. Axiom
Hometown: Seattle, Washington
Height: 6' 1"   Weight: 192 lbs
Eyes: Brown   Hair: None

Super capabilities: Super intelligence; able to shrink to the size of an atom; sunglasses give x-ray vision; lab coat allows for travel through time and space.

Origin: Since birth, Max Axiom seemed destined for greatness. His mother, a marine biologist, taught her son about the mysteries of the sea. His father, a nuclear physicist and volunteer park ranger, schooled Max on the wonders of earth and sky.

One day on a wilderness hike, a megacharged lightning bolt struck Max with blinding fury. When he awoke, Max discovered a newfound energy and set out to learn as much about science as possible. He traveled the globe earning degrees in every aspect of the field. Upon his return, he was ready to share his knowledge and new identity with the world. He had become Max Axiom, Super Scientist.

combustion (kuhm-BUS-chuhn)—the process of burning a fuel with air

compression (kuhm-PRESH-uhn)—the reduction of the volume of a system by applying a force

cylinder (SI-luhn-duhr)—a hollow area inside an engine in which fuel burns to create power

emissions (ee-MI-shuhnz)—gases and particles released into the air by an engine

exhaust (eg-ZAWST)—the waste gases produced by an engine

horsepower (HORSS-pou-ur)—a unit for measuring the power of an engine

hybrid (HYE-brid)—a mix of two different types of technologies; hybrid engines run on electricity and gasoline or diesel fuel

ignite (ig-NITE)—to start combustion

lubrication (loo-bruh-KAY-shuhn)—the addition of a substance, such as oil, to reduce friction and heat generated by parts rubbing against each other

octane number (OK-tang NUM-bur)—a measure of how much a fuel can be compressed before it ignites

piston (PIS-tuhn)—part of an engine that moves up and down within a cylinder

rotor (ROH-tur)—the part of an engine or other machine that turns or rotates

valve (VALV)—a movable part that controls the flow of liquid or gas through a pipe or opening

READ MORE

Bearce, Stephanie. *All about Electric and Hybrid Cars (And Who's Driving Them).* Tell Your Parents. Hockessin, Del.: Mitchell Lane Publishers, 2010.

Eason, Sarah. *How Does a Car Work?* How Does It Work? New York: Gareth Stevens Pub., 2010.

Kenney, Karen Latchana. *Shop Tech: The Science of Cars.* Everyday Science. Mankato, Minn.: Compass Point Books, 2011.

INTERNET SITES

FactHound offers a safe, fun way to find Internet sites related to this book. All sites on FactHound have been researched by our staff.

Here's all you do:

Visit *www.facthound.com*

Type in this code: 9781476531038

Check out projects, games and lots more at
www.capstonekids.com

Index

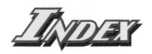